Games for
Grammar
Practice

A resource book of grammar games and interactive activities

ESL Teacher
Ms. Strauss

Maria Lucia Zaorob
and Elizabeth Chin

CAMBRIDGE
UNIVERSITY PRESS

PUBLISHED BY THE PRESS SYNDICATE OF THE UNIVERSITY OF CAMBRIDGE
The Pitt Building, Trumpington Street, Cambridge, United Kingdom

CAMBRIDGE UNIVERSITY PRESS
The Edinburgh Building, Cambridge CB2 2RU, UK
40 West 20th Street, New York, NY 10011–4211, USA
477 Williamstown Road, Port Melbourne, VIC 3207, Australia
Ruiz de Alarcón 13, 28014 Madrid, Spain
Dock House, The Waterfront, Cape Town 8001, South Africa

http://www.cambridge.org

First published 2001
Fifth printing 2005

Printed in the United Kingdom at the University Press, Cambridge

Typeface Formata Light 9/13.5pt.   System QuarkXPress®   [GECKO]

A catalogue record for this book is available from the British Library

Library of Congress Cataloguing in Publication data

ISBN 0 521 663423

Introduction

Games for Grammar Practice is a carefully designed selection of over forty games and activities for intensive and interactive grammar practice with basic to advanced learners of English. Because it follows closely the grammar syllabus of most EFL/ESL courses, it is a most useful complement to many course and grammar books in use today.

THE IDEAS BEHIND THE ACTIVITIES

Cooperative learning You will probably notice that, in most games, knowing the language is not the main factor that leads to winning; actually, luck, strategy and creativity play important roles. This has been done on purpose to foster a cooperative rather than competitive atmosphere, and to make sure weaker learners can also participate and win. Also, in some of the games there is no winner at all.

Teaching, not testing The activities in the book are meant to give learners an opportunity to practise and experiment with language. For this reason many of them present a lot of input while requiring relatively little production in the target structure. This encourages learners to concentrate on processing the meaning of target structures instead of pressuring them to produce such constructions before they are ready to.

Self and peer correction Our experience tells us that self and peer correction are often more effective than teacher correction in helping students to take responsibility for their own learning. Thus most of the game rules and activity procedures urge the participants to monitor their own as well as their peers' language production.

Practice The activities have been designed to make sure that learners get plenty of practice in the target structures.

Personalization There is plenty of room for learners to establish rapport with their classmates by sharing their experiences, values and beliefs.

Oral interaction All the activities are interactive to encourage learners to attend to meaning and form as they interpret and produce language.

Information gap If exchange of information is one of the basic reasons why people communicate in real life, then classroom activities should also urge learners to seek and provide information.

Task-orientation As in real life, learners will be using the information obtained from others to accomplish tasks.

Variety You will find a lot of variety as to context, activity type, type of interaction and materials, because novelty helps to sustain interest.

Enjoyment Fun and pleasure in learning are probably the strongest motivation factors. In our activities, they take the form of challenge, humour and acknowledgement of learners' creativity.

PRACTICAL TIPS

Re-using the material It is probably best to have the boards and cards laminated. However, as this may turn out to be quite expensive, you may instead photocopy the pages directly onto cardboard or paste the photocopies onto sheets of cardboard. As for the boards, another inexpensive solution is to keep them inside plastic bags.

Sorting out sets of cards This task will be much easier for you and your students if you distinguish the sets by colour. So, either photocopy the pages onto coloured sheets or draw straight lines right across or down the back of the sheets with coloured felt-tipped pens before cutting up the cards. You may also want to store them away in coloured envelopes or bags.

Substituting material In case you do not have enough counters, use coloured paper clips instead. They are easy to find and inexpensive.

Preparing for activities Read the instructions carefully and make sure you have the necessary material. Either explain or demonstrate how the game or activity works. Use L1 if necessary, especially with beginners. Note that the vocabulary lists provided in the instruction sheets reflect what we think might be new to students. Always check the boards, cards, or grids for vocabulary items, and pre-teach them if necessary.

Thanks and acknowledgements

Our special thanks go to Maria Cristina de Araujo Asperti, who contributed with invaluable suggestions, endless patience, encouragement and friendship, and to Carlos Barbisan for his interest and support.

We also want to thank all our students who helped to test the material in this book, and thus contributed to its improvement.

The authors and publishers would like to thank the following individuals for their help in commenting on the material, piloting it with their students and for the invaluable feedback which they provided:

Jania Barrell, UK; Sue Bremner, Singapore; Therese Elliot, France; Andrea Paul, Japan; Wayne Trotman, Turkey.

Illustrations: Kathy Baxendale (pp. 13, 91); Belinda Evans (pp. 11, 27, 53, 113); Martin Fish (pp. 17, 18, 65); Gecko Ltd (pp. 9, 31, 44, 45, 46, 51, 67, 95); Melanie Hardy (p. 65); Phil Healey (p. 21); Amanda McPhail (pp. 15, 23, 88, 110); Ian Mitchell (pp. 64, 107, 108); Rhiannon Powell (p. 25); Nick Schon (pp. 39, 63, 105); Lisa Smith (pp. 28, 29, 76); Shaun Williams (p. 79).

Text design: Gecko Ltd.

Page make up: Gecko Ltd.

Cover illustration: Jamel Akib

Games for Grammar Practice

Map of the book

KEY: B = BEGINNER; E = ELEMENTARY; P = PRE-INTERMEDIATE; I = INTERMEDIATE; U = UPPER-INTERMEDIATE; A = ADVANCED

Map of the book

1.1 Balloon tours

Language focus

Present simple of *be*
in statements and
wh-questions

Level

Beginner

Type

Information pool

Topic

Countries

Interaction

Pairs

Time

10–15 minutes

Material

Worksheets A and B

Vocabulary

Names of countries: *France, Spain, Australia, USA, Belgium, Mexico*
Wh-questions: *where, what*
Prepositions: *from, in, at*

Comments

This game provides contextualized practice with statements and wh-questions contrasting 3rd person singular and plural of *be*. Students are given a task which they can only accomplish by interacting orally with classmates, that is, by requesting and providing information, and then making decisions based on the information obtained.

Language output

A: *Where is/are (name) from?*
B: *He/she/they is/are from (country).*
A: *What hotel is/are he/she/they in?*
B: *He/she/they is/are at (hotel).*

Procedures

1 Before class, take copies of the worksheet and cut them in half as indicated. In class, give out worksheet A to half of the class, and worksheet B to the other half. Pair off students with worksheets A and B.

2 Elicit the questions and answers in **Language output** using the worksheets. If you like, write a skeleton of the dialogue on the board.

3 Set the situation and the task by telling your students the following: *You work for Prime Balloon Tours. The company has three balloons for tours over the city, and three tour guides: one speaks English, one speaks French, and the other speaks Spanish. Your task is to decide firstly which tourists should go in which balloon, and secondly how many hotels each guide needs to stop at to pick up tourists. Talk to your partners first to get the information you need to do the task.*

4 Doing the activity:

 ▶ Without looking at each other's worksheet, students ask and answer questions and complete their respective charts.
 ▶ When they have finished, they answer questions 1 and 2 on their worksheets, together.
 ▶ Check their answers or decisions with the whole class.

B

Prime Balloon Tours

TOURISTS	COUNTRY	HOTEL
John Smith	USA	The Queen's Plaza
Mr and Mrs Dupont		
Julio Banderas		
Marie Delon	Belgium	The Royal Inn
Jose and Pepe Garcia	Mexico	The Palace
Kathy and Fred Brown		

1 In which balloon should the tourists go? Write the names of the tourists under the appropriate balloon.

_____ _____ _____

2 How many hotels does each guide need to stop at to pick up tourists?

- ✂ - - -

A

Prime Balloon Tours

TOURISTS	COUNTRY	HOTEL
John Smith		
Mr and Mrs Dupont	France	The Royal Inn
Julio Banderas	Spain	The Palace
Marie Delon		
Jose and Pepe Garcia		
Kathy and Fred Brown	Australia	The Bridge House

1 In which balloon should the tourists go? Write the names of the tourists under the appropriate balloon.

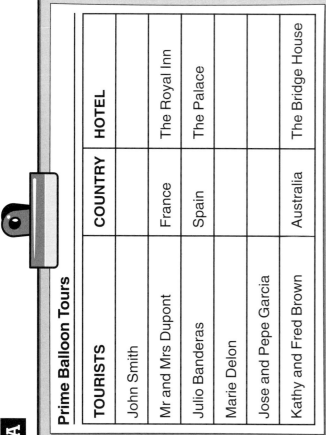

_____ _____ _____

2 How many hotels does each guide need to stop at to pick up tourists?

1.2 A day at home

Present continuous in statements and questions

Level

Elementary

Type

Board game

Topic

Activities done at home

Interaction

Pairs

Time

10–20 minutes

Material

Board (one per pair), counters (four per student)

Vocabulary

Parts of the house: *bathroom, bedroom, backyard, dining room, garden, basement, kitchen, attic, living room*

Verbs: referring to activities associated with the various parts of the house

Comments

Adapted from *Achi*, an African game which resembles tic-tac-toe but also incorporates movement, this game is designed for intensive practice with the present continuous in wh-questions and statements to describe ongoing activities. Because it provides a unified context, learners can integrate grammar and vocabulary practice. Winning the game requires language accuracy, creativity and strategic skill.

Language output

A: *What are you doing in the kitchen/backyard?*

B: *I'm doing the dishes/washing the dog.*

Procedures

1 Pair off students, and give out the material. **Note:** If you don't have enough counters, cut out the black and white squares below the board, and use them instead.

2 Go over the parts of the house shown on the board, and elicit activities that might be done in each part. If you wish, write the vocabulary on the blackboard. Model the target language shown in *Language output*, and demonstrate the game a couple of times.

3 Playing the game:

▶ Objective of the game: align one's counters in a horizontal, vertical or diagonal row of three.

▶ The game begins with student B choosing the spot where he or she wants to place a counter. Then student A asks an appropriate question, as shown in *Language output*. If student B gives an appropriate and correct answer, he or she may place the counter in the chosen spot. Otherwise, no counter goes on the board.

▶ Players take turns doing this until one of them forms a row of three with his or her counters, or until all the counters have been placed on the board.

▶ If no one has formed a row of three and all the counters have been placed on the board, players can once more attempt to form such a row by moving their counters along the lines into the empty spots, one at a time, and interacting as shown above. **Note:** They are not allowed to repeat an answer that has already been given.

▶ The game ends when either one manages to form a horizontal, vertical or diagonal row with his or her counters. As this game depends a lot on the players' strategic skills, it may last anything from two to five minutes. Let them play several times for further practice.

Variations

1 To practise vocabulary related to other activities, replace the parts of the house on the board with other places, e.g. *bank, school, petrol station, post office*, etc.

2 For practice with the various persons and subject-verb agreement, use the spare counters and write on them: *Your mother / You / Your sisters / Your grandpa* etc. The language output will then change to, e.g. *What's your mother doing in the kitchen? She's feeding the cats.*

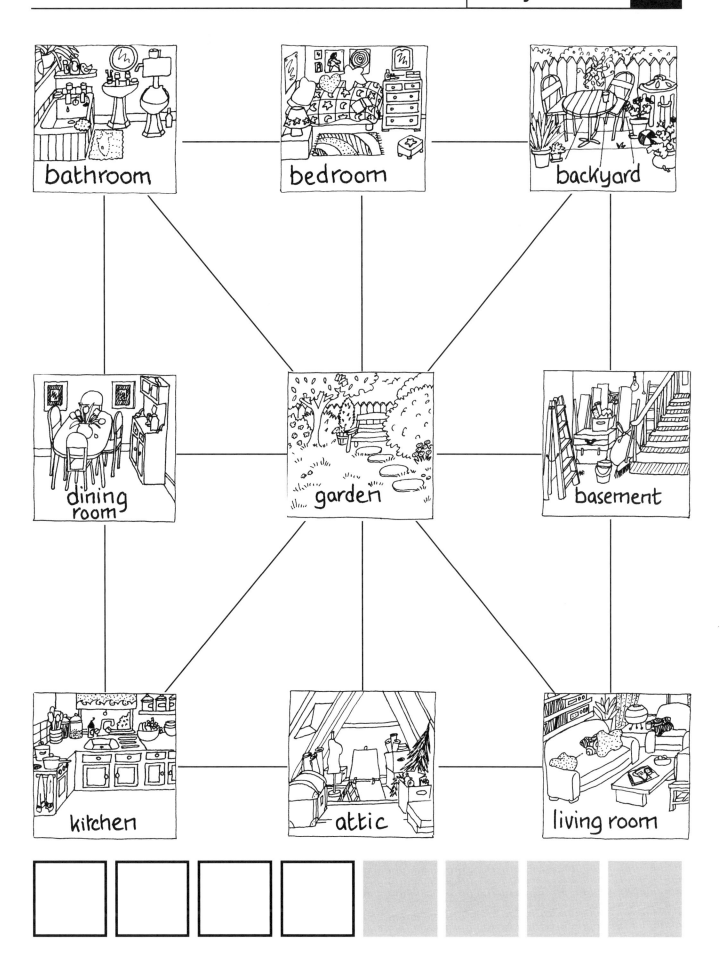

1.3 Looking for a flatmate

Language focus

Present simple in statements and questions

Level

Elementary

Type

Interview

Topic

Habits and routines

Interaction

Pairs

Time

20 minutes

Material

Worksheet (one per student)

Vocabulary

Verbs: *have, cook, get up, take, go, get back, do*

Nouns: *pet, car, hobbies, shower, work, home, dinner, evening, activities, weekend*

Comments

In this activity, students will have intensive controlled practice with the simple present in statements and questions involving the 2nd person singular, plus statements in the 3rd person singular. This is an excellent opportunity for elementary students to get to know one another and talk about themselves while interacting to accomplish the task proposed.

Language output

Phase I A: *Do you have a pet?*
B: *Yes, I do. I have a turtle.*
A: *What time do you get up?*
B: *I usually get up at 7:00.*

Phase II T: *Who do you prefer as a flatmate?*
St: *I prefer (name).*
T: *Why?*
St: *Because he / she cooks / doesn't have a pet.*

Procedures

Phase I

1 Introduce the topic of sharing rooms or flats. Elicit problems that people might have, and what it is important to check before choosing a flatmate.

2 Set the context and the task by telling students: *You are looking for a flatmate. You are going to interview two friends to decide who will be your flatmate.*

3 Hand out the worksheets, and elicit the questions associated with the cues given. Emphasize the correct use of the auxiliary *do*. Encourage students to come up with other questions that are important to them and allow them to omit any questions they do not consider important.

4 Doing the activity:

▶ Individually, students complete the first column of the chart with information about themselves.
▶ In pairs, students ask and answer questions to complete the second column.
▶ Students switch pairs, and repeat this last procedure to fill out the third column.
▶ Give students a few minutes to decide who they prefer as a flatmate and why.

Phase II

1 With the whole class, elicit some of your students' choices and reasons. Use this opportunity to introduce the 3rd person singular *-s* ending in statements.

2 Have students report their choices and reasons to the class.

Facts

have a pet

have a car

have any hobbies

cook

You	Student A	Student B

Daily routine

get up

take a shower

go to work

get back home

have dinner

evening activities

weekend activities

You	Student A	Student B

1.4 Lend a hand

Language focus

Present simple 3rd person singular in statements and questions

Level

Pre-intermediate

Type

Problem solving

Topic

Age, occupations and hobbies

Interaction

Pairs

Time

20 minutes

Material

Worksheets A and B

Vocabulary

Professions: *reporter, cook, farmer, teacher*

Activities: *cook the meals, wash the dishes, clean the bathrooms, take care of the little kids, entertain the teenagers, give swimming lessons, look after the horses, take care of the garden*

Hobbies: *(go) swimming, (do) gardening, (go) horseback riding, (do) handicraft*

Comments

This contextualized and task-oriented information gap activity asks learners to collect information and make decisions while providing them with an opportunity to practise asking and answering questions involving the present simple 3rd person singular. It can also be used to introduce or review collocations such as *go swimming*, and some phrasal verbs, e.g. *look after.*

Language output

A: *How old is Sharon Miles?*
B: *She's 28.*
A: *What does she do?*
B: *She's a reporter.*
A: *Where does she work?*
B: *She works at/for MTV.*
A: *What does she do in her free time?*
B: *She goes swimming.*

Procedures

Phase I

1 Before class, take copies of the worksheet and cut them in half as indicated. In class, hand out worksheet A to half of the class, and worksheet B to the other half.

2 Set the context and the task by telling the class: *You are organizers of a summer camp for homeless children. You have a list of volunteers. Your task is to decide what you are going to do and what the volunteers are each going to do.*

3 Individually, students read the list of chores and write their names next to the two chores they want to do.

4 Pair off students with worksheets A and B to find out what their partners want to do. Write *What do you want to do? I want to …* on the board if necessary. In case of conflicting interests, let them sort it out with whatever language they can use.

Phase II

1 Using the worksheets, elicit the questions and answers in **Language output** above.

2 In pairs, students get from their partners the missing information on the volunteers.

3 Students then decide, in pairs and together, what the best chores are for each volunteer.

4 If you wish, regroup students so they can report on and discuss their decisions with other peers.

B

Tasks

cook the meals

wash the dishes

clean the bathrooms

take care of the little kids

entertain the teenagers

give swimming lessons

look after the horses

take care of the garden

Who?

_____

_____

_____

_____

Lend a hand
Help us help our children

Name: Phil Lee
Category: Volunteer
Age: 29
Job: cook
Place of Work: Mr Chow's
Hobbies: gardening

Lend a hand
Help us help our children

Name: Sergei Seibel
Category: Volunteer
Age:
Job:
Place of Work:
Hobbies:

Lend a hand
Help us help our children

Name: Sharon Miles
Category: Volunteer
Age:
Job:
Place of Work:
Hobbies:

Lend a hand
Help us help our children

Name: Maria Fernandez
Category: Volunteer
Age: 33
Job: teacher
Place of Work: Kinnelon High
Hobbies: handicraft

✂

A

Tasks

cook the meals

wash the dishes

clean the bathrooms

take care of the little kids

entertain the teenagers

give swimming lessons

look after the horses

take care of the garden

Who?

_____

_____

_____

_____

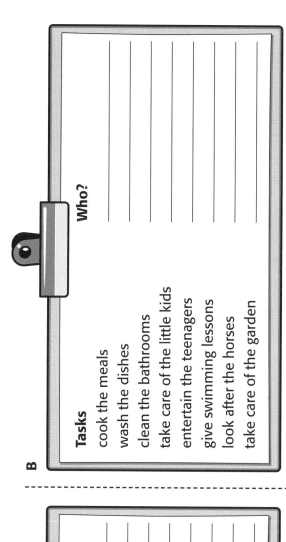

Lend a hand
Help us help our children

Name: Phil Lee
Category: Volunteer
Age:
Job:
Place of Work:
Hobbies:

Lend a hand
Help us help our children

Name: Sergei Seibel
Category: Volunteer
Age: 53
Job: farmer
Place of Work: Sunny Farm
Hobbies: horse riding

Lend a hand
Help us help our children

Name: Sharon Miles
Category: Volunteer
Age: 28
Job: Reporter
Place of Work: MTV
Hobbies: swimming

Lend a hand
Help us help our children

Name: Maria Fernandez
Category: Volunteer
Age:
Job:
Place of Work:
Hobbies:

1.5 Time and again

Language focus

Adverbials of frequency

Level

Elementary or
pre-intermediate

Type

Betting game

Topic

Activities and events

Interaction

Groups of three or four

Time

20–30 minutes

Material

Two sets of cards per
group

Vocabulary

Activities: Any activity students can think of for a given picture, e.g. picture 1 may generate: *go swimming, swim in the sea/a lake/a river, swim across the English Channel*, etc.

Adverbials of frequency: *every day, more than once a day, quite often, almost every day, about once a week, sometimes, a couple of times a month, once or twice a year, not very often, hardly ever, seldom, never*

Comments

This game gives learners an opportunity to practise asking questions with *how often*, and answering them with adverbials of frequency, while using a lot of vocabulary related to general activities and events. It is quite challenging and fun in that players must be able to anticipate their opponents' answers in order to lay down their cards and win the game. That means knowing their classmates well and being able to use their picture prompts creatively.

Language output

A: *How often do you do your homework?*
B: *I seldom do my homework.*

Procedures

1 Before class, cut out one set of picture cards and one set of frequency cards for each group.

2 Elicit and model the language in **Language output** several times to make sure students are able to formulate the questions and use the adverbials of frequency.

3 Divide the class into groups and hand out the material.

4 Demonstrate being student A, using different adverbials. Show them how they can use the picture prompts creatively to generate the adverbials they want, e.g. *How often do you go to the beach in the summer? About once a week. How often does your grandmother wear a bikini on the beach? Never.* Note that some of the adverbial cards are quite specific, e.g. *once or twice a year*, while others are underspecified, e.g. *often*. This will encourage discussion and help learners understand that the meaning of some adverbials of frequency may vary according to the activity they refer to, e.g. *often* in *I often catch a cold* (perhaps several times a year) and *I often have a holiday in the Bahamas* (perhaps once every two years).

5 Playing the game:
- Players shuffle the picture cards and place them face down in the middle. Then, they shuffle the frequency cards and deal them out evenly.
- The first player turns up a picture card from the pile and decides (a) which one of his or her frequency cards to use, and (b) who the *'How often …?'* question will be directed to. The question must involve the picture on the picture card that the player has just picked from the pile, and the purpose is to get an answer containing the adverbial on the selected adverbial card.
- The player then formulates the question. If the respondent uses the adverbial on the selected frequency card or some other adverbial that the group accepts as being equivalent, then the first player may discard it. Otherwise, he or she keeps the card without showing it to the group.
- The first player to get rid of all of his or her cards wins the game.

Picture cards

Picture cards

From *Games for Grammar Practice* © Cambridge University Press 2001 *PHOTOCOPIABLE*

Frequency cards

every day	more than once a day	quite often
almost every day	about once a week	sometimes
a couple of times a month	once or twice a year	not very often
hardly ever	seldom	never

2.1 Gotcha!

Language focus

Simple past of regular and irregular verbs

Level

Elementary

Type

Questions and answers

Topic

Activities and events

Interaction

Pairs

Time

10 minutes

Material

Worksheets A and B, dice (two per pair)

Vocabulary

Verbs: *meet, buy, see, arrive, go, celebrate, eat, do, get up, come, visit, brush, read, talk, have, spend, leave, wash, wear, give*

Comments

The objective of this game is to give learners plenty of wh-questions in the simple past as input, plus an opportunity to practise the simple past of regular and irregular verbs in statements. Even though it is quite controlled, this activity urges learners to talk about themselves, and to monitor their own language as well as their peers, as they can only score with accurate answers.

Language output

A: *Where did you spend your last holiday?*

B: *I spent my last holiday on my uncle's farm.*

Procedures

1 Before class, take copies of the worksheet and cut them in half as indicated.

2 Elicit and model the language output by asking students several wh-questions in the simple past and requiring their answers to be correct, especially with regard to verb form.

3 Hand out worksheet A to half of the class, and worksheet B to the other half. Pair off students with worksheets A and B, and give two dice to each pair.

4 Playing the game:

   ▶ The game begins with student B casting the dice and adding the numbers rolled. Then student A asks the question that corresponds to that total on his or her own worksheet. For example, if B rolls the dice and they total 8, student A asks question 8 on his or her worksheet, which is: *Where did you spend your last holiday?*

   ▶ If student B answers correctly, he or she blasts that question from student A's worksheet. Otherwise, that question remains active and can be asked again at some other turn, depending on the dice. In other words, because incorrect answers are rejected rather than corrected immediately, players are given an opportunity for self-correction at some other point in the game.

   ▶ Players take turns doing this. The first player to blast all of the opponents' questions wins the game.

Variations

If you want students to practise formulating the questions rather than just reading them, replace the questions on the worksheets with cues.

Note on material

If you are short of dice, hand out one to each pair and have them roll it twice.

A

4

What did you wear to school/work yesterday?

3

What did you give your mother for Christmas?

2

How did you go home yesterday?

8

Where did you spend your last holiday?

7

What did you have for breakfast last Sunday?

6

When did you last wash your hair?

5

What time did you leave home this morning?

12

Who did you talk with last night?

11

What did you read last weekend?

10

How many times did you brush your teeth yesterday?

9

What did you do last weekend?

9

Where did you meet your best friend?

10

What did you buy last week?

11

When did you first see the sea?

12

What time did you arrive home last Saturday?

5

Who did you visit last weekend?

6

How many times did you go to the movies last month?

7

Where did you celebrate your last birthday?

8

What did you eat last night?

2

What did you do yesterday?

3

What time did you get up this morning?

4

How did you come here today?

B

2.2 Everyday hazards

Language focus

Simple past and past continuous

Level

Intermediate

Type

Story telling

Topic

Funny accidents

Interaction

Groups of three or four

Time

20 minutes

Material

Set of cards
(one per group)

Vocabulary

Verbs: *hang around, walk into, look at, fight, ride, fall into, run over, go too fast, lean over*

Nouns: *moped, pothole, traffic officer, bike, jogger, ducks, pond, rail*

Comments

In this activity learners will be practising the simple past and past continuous as well as some phrasal verbs, as they compose story lines with the bits of information given. Unlike many other storytelling activities, there is no fixed story line in this case. Learners are free to link the circumstances and events in any logical way they wish in order to create meaning.

Language output

Fiona was hanging around in the mall last Saturday. She suddenly walked into a huge Christmas tree right in the middle of a hall, knocking down the tree and decorations, because she was looking at two people fighting and didn't see where she was going. She quickly picked up the tree, and pretended to be the mall's decorator, because she felt everyone was looking at her.

Procedures

1 Before class, cut out one set of cards for every group of three or four students.

2 Begin to model the language by telling your class a funny accident you have had, similar to the one in **Language output**, drawing attention to the simple past and past continuous forms in your story. Then get a couple of students to tell their stories, and explore the details with questions, while encouraging the use of the correct verb forms.

3 Divide the class into groups and hand out the material.

4 Doing the activity:

▶ Players shuffle the cards and deal them out evenly.

▶ Players take turns laying down their cards, one at a time, in the centre of the table to compose four story lines. The stories belong to the entire group, that is, everyone may compose and change them.

▶ Rules of the game:
→ Players may only begin a story line if they have a character card to lay down.
→ They may add cards to any existing stories on the table provided that the stories continue to make sense.
→ They may change the sequence of cards within any story line or move cards from one story to another in order to accommodate new cards.
→ The player who wants to lay down a *So … The end* card will have to invent its content, that is, the end of the story. This may be done at any time during the game, and other players may continue inserting other cards in the middle of the story, but they may not change its ending.
→ If a player cannot lay down any of his or her cards, he or she says *I pass*.

▶ The winner is the first player to get rid of all of his or her cards.

Follow-up

Groups choose their favourite story and tell it to the rest of the class.

So …	The End	looking at two people fighting	walked into a huge Christmas tree	hanging around	in the mall
So …	The End	looking at a good-looking traffic officer	fell into a pothole	riding a moped	in the street
So …	The End	going too fast	ran over a jogger	riding a bike	in a park
So …	The End	leaning over the rail	fell into the pond	looking at the ducks	at the zoo

Fiona

Tina

Dan

Brad

2.3 Sweet memories

Language focus

Used to

Level

Intermediate or upper-intermediate

Type

Board game

Topic

Growing-up memories

Interaction

Groups of two to six

Time

20–30 minutes

Material

Board and dice (one per group), counters (one per student)

Vocabulary

Verbs: *grow up, fall down, break, fight with, fail, go on a trip, have a date*

Nouns: *childhood memory, toy, tree house, pet, (school) subject, complaints, idol, hero, date, curfew, school dance*

Comments

This game provides a lot of input and intensive practice with a wide range of verbs in the simple past and habitual past with *used to*. Because the subject of childhood and teenage memories is so close to everyone's heart, the game promotes a lot of conversation and better student rapport. As such, it should be reserved for the more communicative end of the lesson and used for fluency building.

Language output

A: *Who did you use to fight with when you were a teenager?*

B: *I used to fight a lot with my sister.*

A: *Why?*

B: *Well, because she used to borrow my clothes without asking me first.*

A: *And who used to win?*

B: *She did, because my mother was always on her side.*

Procedures

1 Prepare questions related to childhood and teenage experiences. Ask one at a time, elicit answers from the class, and continue the conversation from there, as shown in **Language output**. Draw students' attention to the meaning and use of *used to*, and contrast it with the simple past if necessary.

2 Divide the class into groups and hand out the material.

3 Playing the game:

> ▶ Players place their counters at the starting point (symbol of birth: the stork) on the board.
>
> ▶ They take turns casting the dice and moving along the board accordingly.
>
> ▶ Whenever a player lands on a square with a question in it, someone in the group asks him or her that question, and the player answers. The group should then explore the topic with further questions, answers, comments, etc. Encourage the appropriate use of the simple past and *used to*.
>
> ▶ Whenever a player lands on one of the squares containing happy or unhappy events of life, he or she must follow the instructions in them.
>
> ▶ The first player to get to (but not beyond) the finishing point (symbol of graduation: the mortarboard) wins the game.

Variations

1 If you are teaching teenagers, change the questions so as to suit their young age.

2 If you want to let your students decide what to talk about and formulate the questions themselves, replace the questions on the board with prompts, e.g. *GROW UP, SCHOOL, TOYS, GAMES, DATING, MOTHER, BROTHERS & SISTERS*, etc.

Note on class size

If students are playing in pairs or groups of three, use coins instead of dice. That way they will move either one square (heads) or two squares (tails), and have more opportunities to talk.

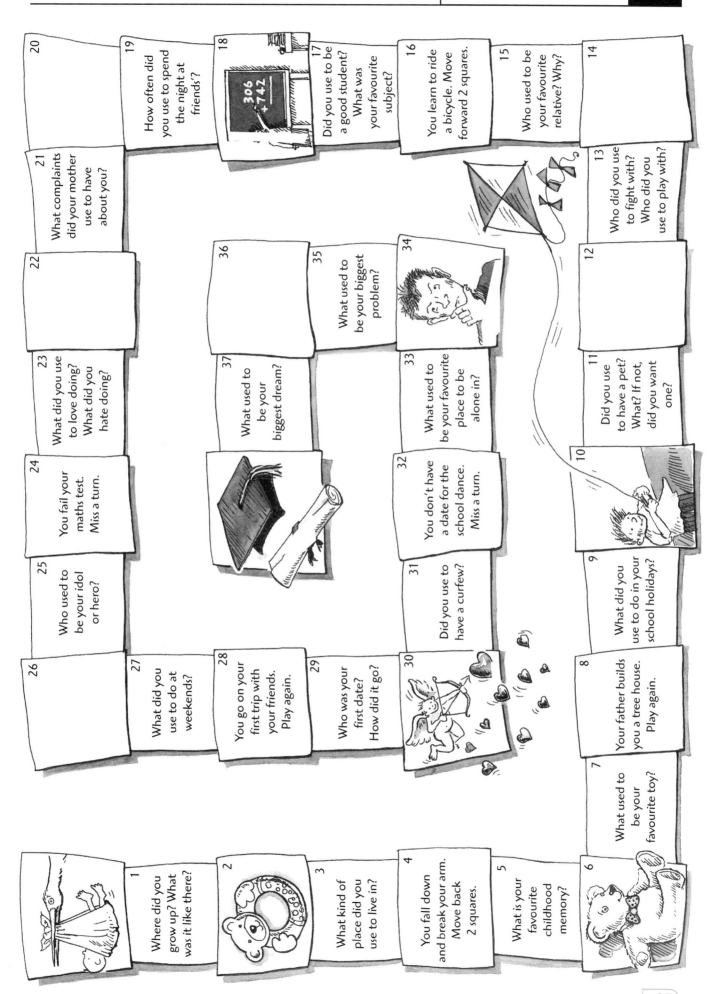

20

19 How often did you use to spend the night at friends'?

18

17 Did you use to be a good student? What was your favourite subject?

16 You learn to ride a bicycle. Move forward 2 squares.

15 Who used to be your favourite relative? Why?

14

21 What complaints did your mother use to have about you?

22

23 What did you use to love doing? What did you hate doing?

24 You fail your maths test. Miss a turn.

25 Who used to be your idol or hero?

26

27 What did you use to do at weekends?

28 You go on your first trip with your friends. Play again.

29 Who was your first date? How did it go?

36

37 What used to be your biggest dream?

35 What used to be your biggest problem?

34

33 What used to be your favourite place to be alone in?

32 You don't have a date for the school dance. Miss a turn.

31 Did you use to have a curfew?

30

13 Who did you use to fight with? Who did you use to play with?

12

11 Did you use to have a pet? What? If not, did you want one?

10

9 What did you use to do in your school holidays?

8 Your father builds you a tree house. Play again.

7 What used to be your favourite toy?

1 Where did you grow up? What was it like there?

2

3 What kind of place did you use to live in?

4 You fall down and break your arm. Move back 2 squares.

5 What is your favourite childhood memory?

6

3.1 Around town

Language focus

Present perfect simple

Level

Intermediate or upper–intermediate

Type

Board game

Topic

Recent experiences or events

Interaction

Groups of two to six

Time

20 minutes

Material

Board, set of cards, and dice (one per group), counters (one per student)

Vocabulary

Mostly prompted by pictures.

Words and expressions on situation cards: *run out of, absent-minded, spilled, tough luck, gone through a red light, fine*

Comments

This game has been designed to relate past events with present results, and to provide much-needed practice of the present perfect simple to express such relationships. The activity is fun in that it stimulates learners' imagination and acknowledges their individual contributions.

Language output

A: *What's happened to Bill?*
B: *He's flat broke/depressed.*
A: *Why/How come?*
B: *Because he has lost all his money in the stock market.*
A: *Gee, that's too bad. What's he going to do now?*
B: *I don't know. Never buy stocks again, I guess.*

Procedures

1 Before class, cut out one set of cards for each group.

2 Write *Bill is depressed* on the board. Elicit possible causes and write them to the left of the sentence, drawing students' attention to the use of the present perfect simple, e.g. *He has lost his job/His girlfriend has left him,* etc. Then elicit plausible future actions that Bill might take. Model the target language with several students.

3 Divide the class into groups and hand out the material.

4 Playing the game:

▶ Players place their counters at START, shuffle the cards and place them face down on the table. There are two kinds of cards. The picture cards depict present results which students must interpret (e.g. *Maria is very happy*) and think of causes for, using the present perfect simple (e.g. *She has been promoted to vice-president*). The situation cards, on the other hand, provide input on the present perfect simple, plus the luck element in the game, for they contain situations and instructions that may lead the player back to the beginning of the board or toss him or her closer to the FINISH point.

▶ The first player casts the dice and moves his or her counter accordingly. If it lands on a shop, nothing happens, but if it lands on a house, the player picks a card and turns it face up so everyone can see what is happening inside the house. If it is a picture card, the person to the left of the player begins interaction with him or her as shown in **Language output**. On the other hand, if it is a situation card, the player simply reads it aloud and follows the instructions on it.

▶ Players take turns proceeding in this way. The first player to get to (but not beyond) the FINISH point wins the game.

Note on group size

If students are playing in pairs or groups of three, use coins instead of dice. That way they will move one square (heads) or two squares (tails), and get more practice.

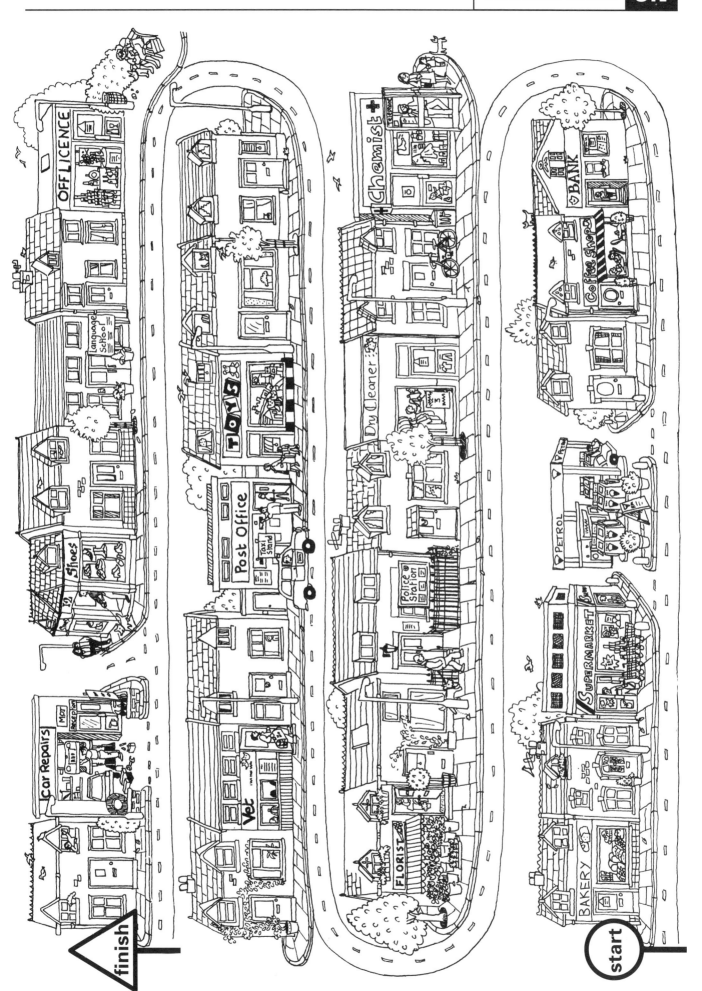

Bill

Jeff

Jessica

Maria

Ted

Rosie

Andrew

Alison
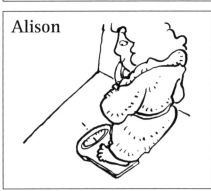

Daniel and Bob

Jane

Alex

John

Susie

Kevin

Ella and Kate

From *Games for Grammar Practice* © Cambridge University Press 2001 **PHOTOCOPIABLE**

Nick	Wendy	Joel

Vicky	Liz	Anne

You've run out of petrol. How can you be so absent-minded? Go to the nearest petrol station.	You haven't eaten anything all day. Aren't you hungry? Go to the coffee shop for a sandwich.	You have spilled coffee all over your new jacket. Take it to the dry cleaner's.
Your sister has just had a baby. How about getting her some flowers? Go to the florist.	Tough luck! You've just missed the bus. Go to the taxi stand in front of the post office.	You have just gone through a red light. What a shame! Go to the bank and pay the fine.
Your cat has fallen off the roof again. You'd better take it to the vet to make sure everything is OK.	Don't forget you've invited friends over for dinner. Go to the supermarket and get something for dessert.	You haven't talked to your mother today. She must be worried! There is a pay phone just outside the chemist.

3.2 Snooping around

Language focus

Present perfect simple
with *ever*

Level

Intermediate to advanced

Type

Truth or dare

Topic

Life experiences

Interaction

Groups of two to six

Time

20–30 minutes

Material

Board, set of cards, dice
(one per group), counters
(one per student)

Vocabulary

Words and expressions: *dangerous sports, act on stage, fancy dress party, fail, contest, raffle, mugged, make a silly mistake, have a crush on, tear out, get blind drunk, sneak away, jump a queue, personal ad, make a hoax call, cheat, search through, belongings, date, naked, flirt, forge, peep through, keyhole, bribe, fortune teller.*

Comments

The purpose here is to provide plenty of input on the present perfect simple + *ever*, to get learners to understand how this tense contrasts with the simple past, and to practise a lot with both. Despite the initial controlled prompt, the activity invites learners to share life experiences and is therefore excellent for generating conversation and building fluency.

Language output

A: *Have you ever been to a fortune teller?*
B: *Yes, I have.*
A: *Why did you go there?*
B: *Well, I wanted to know when I would find a girlfriend.*

Procedures

1 This game includes three sets of cards, marked 1 to 3, containing questions graded from the least to the most controversial. So, look through them and pick the set or the cards that best suit(s) your students' age and culture. Then, cut out one set of 14 or more cards for each group.

2 Model the language by asking your class *Have you ever…?* questions and developing conversation from there. The aim is to point out the use of the present perfect simple versus the simple past.

3 Divide the class into groups and hand out the material.

4 Playing the game:

▶ Players shuffle the cards, place them face down in the centre of the board, and distribute their counters among the four corners.

▶ They take turns casting the dice and moving their counters accordingly as indicated by the arrows. Whenever a player lands on a balloon, he or she wins the right to pick a card and ask anyone in the group the 'nosy' question on it, plus one other related question to satisfy his or her curiosity.

▶ The winner is the first player to get back to his or her starting corner. Alternatively, you may let them play for as long as they like or until you think they have had enough practice.

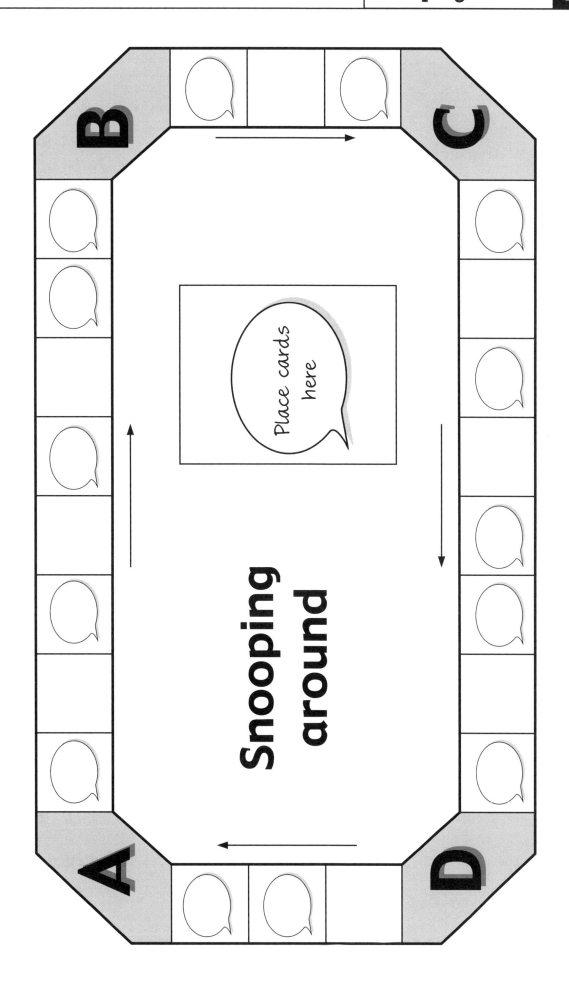

Cards 1

Have you ever eaten anything usually considered strange?

Have you ever fallen asleep at a party?

Have you ever tried any dangerous sports?

Have you ever acted on stage?

Have you ever written a poem?

Have you ever gone to a fancy dress party?

Have you ever failed a course or important test?

Have you ever done volunteer work?

Have you ever lost your documents?

Have you ever missed a plane?

Have you ever made a major change in your life?

Have you ever written to a newspaper or magazine?

Have you ever won anything in a contest or raffle?

Have you ever found anything valuable?

Have you ever been robbed or mugged?

Cards 2

Have you ever made a really silly mistake?	Have you ever followed anybody?	Have you ever borrowed anybody's clothes without asking?
Have you ever had a crush on a teacher?	Have you ever torn out pages of somebody's book or magazine?	Have you ever been blind drunk?
Have you ever broken anything and just sneaked away?	Have you ever jumped a queue?	Have you ever lied about your age?
Have you ever written an anonymous letter?	Have you ever replied to a personal ad in a newspaper?	Have you ever written a love letter to anyone?
Have you ever taken anything from a hotel?	Have you ever gone to a party without being invited?	Have you ever made a hoax call?

Cards 3

Have you ever stolen anything from a shop?

Have you ever received too much change and kept it?

Have you ever cheated in an exam?

Have you ever secretly searched through somebody's belongings?

Have you ever lied to your parents?

Have you ever dated more than one person at the same time?

Have you ever gone swimming naked?

Have you ever flirted with a friend's date?

Have you ever forged somebody's signature?

Have you ever opened somebody's mail?

Have you ever written on a bathroom wall?

Have you ever changed prices in a shop?

Have you ever peeped through a keyhole?

Have you ever tried to bribe anybody?

Have you ever been to a fortune teller?

3.3 Before or after?

Language focus
Past perfect simple

Level
Intermediate or upper-intermediate

Type
Card game

Topic
Causes and consequences

Interaction
Groups of four or five

Time
15–20 minutes

Material
Two sets of cards per group

Vocabulary

Conjunctions: *as, since, because, so*

Words and expressions: *be fired, fail, flat broke, know your way around, fall asleep, oversleep, miss class, overdrawn*

Comments

This game offers plenty of input contrasting the past perfect simple and the simple past. There are visual clues as to the relation between these two tenses and the order of events on a time line in cause-and-effect statements. The activity focuses on both meaning and form, while encouraging learners to monitor their peers and negotiate group consensus.

Language output

As/since/because I hadn't slept all night, I was very tired.
I was very tired because I hadn't slept all night.
I was very tired, so I fell asleep.

Procedures

1 Before class, cut out one set of situation cards and one set of causes-and-consequences cards for each group.

2 Model the language by writing *I had a fight with my sister last month* on the board. Elicit possible causes, e.g. *She had borrowed my bike and scratched it* and list them on the left. Elicit possible consequences or effects, e.g. *I didn't talk to her for three days* and list these on the right. Have students combine the ideas into compound sentences with the right conjunctions, paying attention to the use of simple past and past perfect simple.

3 Divide the class into groups and hand out the material.

4 Playing the game:
   ‣ Players shuffle the situation cards and place them face down on the table. Then, they shuffle the causes-and-consequences cards and deal these out evenly.
   ‣ One player turns up a situation card. Whoever is holding a card expressing a plausible cause or consequence for that situation may place it, accordingly, to the left or right of the situation card, and connects the ideas with the right conjunction.
   ‣ The group then decides whether the connection is plausible or not. If it is, the card placed on the table is considered discarded; if not, the player must take it back.
   ‣ For any given situation, all players may discard as many cards as they like, provided the connections are plausible.
   ‣ The first player to get rid of all of his or her cards wins the game.

Note on language

You may want to point out to your students that, in spoken language, it is more common to invert the clauses when the conjunction *because* is used, e.g. *I was very tired because I hadn't slept all night* but the verb forms and meaning remain unchanged.

situation cards

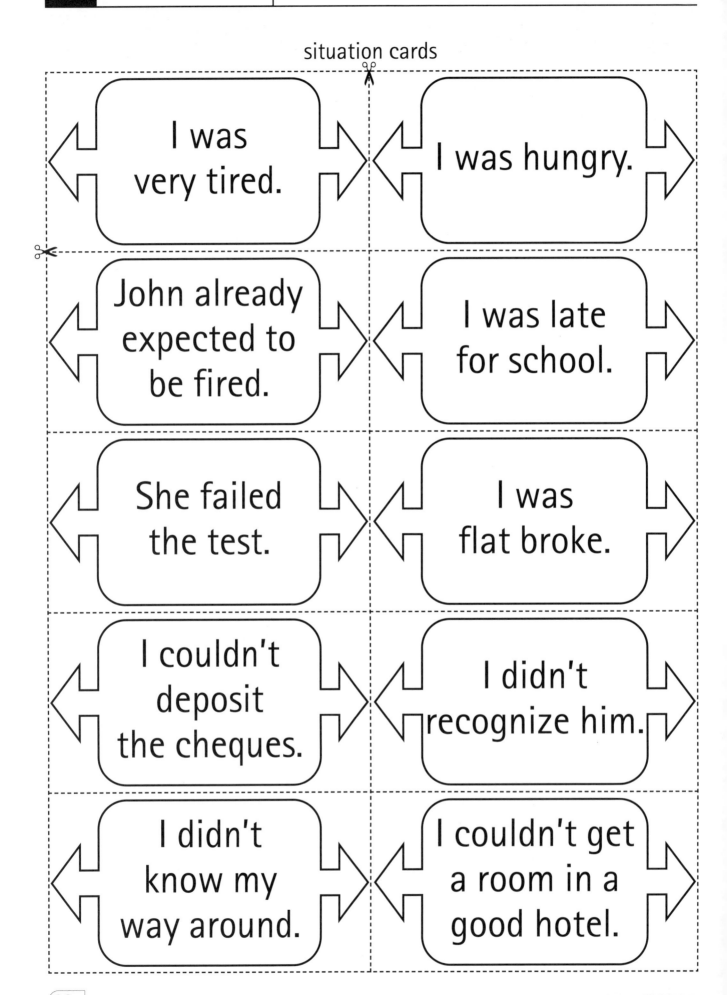

I was
very tired.

I was hungry.

John already
expected to
be fired.

I was late
for school.

She failed
the test.

I was
flat broke.

I couldn't
deposit
the cheques.

I didn't
recognize him.

I didn't
know my
way around.

I couldn't get
a room in a
good hotel.

causes-and-consequences cards

I went to McDonald's.	I missed my first class.	I borrowed some money from my mother.	I didn't talk to him.	I had to stay with friends.
I hadn't had lunch.	I had overslept.	I had spent all my salary on new clothes.	We hadn't met for many years.	I hadn't made reservations.
I fell asleep in the middle of the concert.	He wasn't surprised.	She decided to study harder next time.	My account was overdrawn.	I got lost.
I hadn't slept all night.	He had lost an important contract.	She hadn't studied much.	The bank had just closed.	I hadn't been there before.

4.1 What on earth ...?

Language focus

Going to

Level

Pre-intermediate or intermediate

Type

Board game

Topic

Intended actions

Interaction

Groups of two to six

Time

20 minutes

Material

Board and dice (one per group), counters (one per student)

Vocabulary

Nouns: *hat, apple, racket, cup, money, shopping bag, books, parcel, aspirin, blackboard, mask, pram, potatoes, magnifying glass, suitcase, broom, bucket, pencil, flowers, popcorn, envelope, bottle, bag of flour, credit card*

Comments

This interactive board game gets learners to associate the expression of intentions with the right future form: *going to*. As it requires players to imagine a variety of actions for each one of the objects depicted on the board, the game can be very stimulating and humorous.

Language output

A: *What on earth are you going to do with that magnifying glass?*

B: *I'm going to look for my contact lenses.*

Procedures

1 Bring to class pictures of objects that are large enough for the whole class to see. Give one of them to a student, step back, and ask: *What on earth are you going to do with that ...?* Elicit an answer from that student and other possible or funny answers from the rest of the class. Draw students' attention to the use and meaning of *going to*. Repeat this procedure to make sure students can use this form appropriately and understand the idea of the game.

2 Divide the class into groups and hand out the material.

3 Playing the game:

▶ Players place their counters at START.

▶ The first player casts the dice and moves his or her counter accordingly. If it lands on a square with an object in it, the person to his or her left initiates interaction with him or her, as shown in *Language output*. If the counter lands on a square with instructions in it, he or she must follow them.

▶ Players take turns proceeding in this way. The first player to get to (but not beyond) the FINISH point wins the game.

Variation

For intermediate students with good vocabulary and to make the game more challenging and humorous, have them come up with unusual actions for the objects, e.g.

A: *What on earth are you going to do with that magnifying glass?*

B: *I'm going to start a camp fire in the garden.*

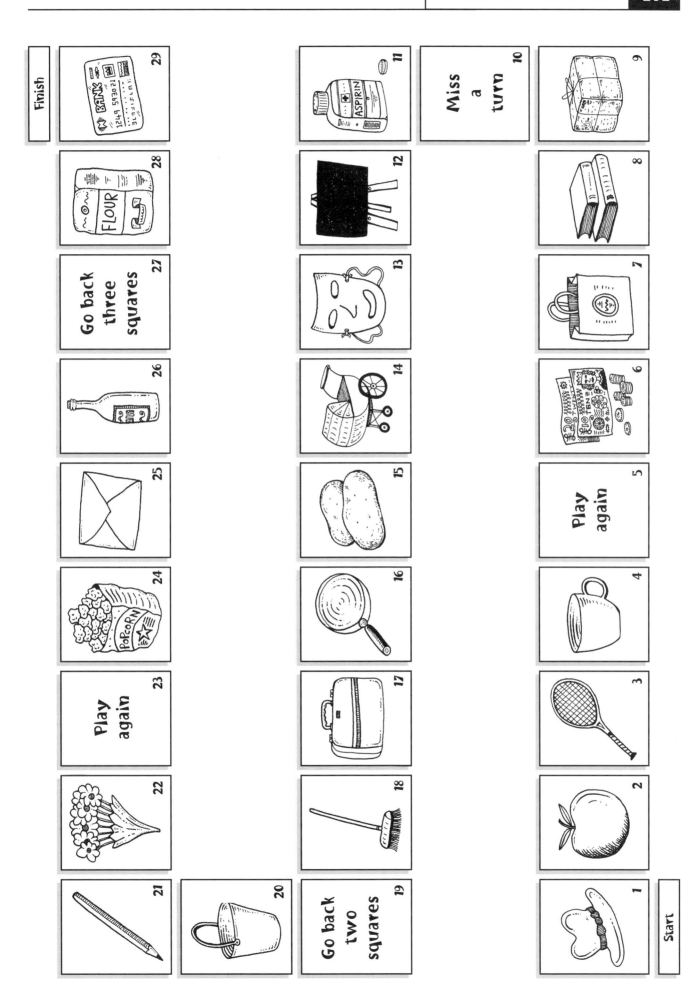

4.2 Make it snappy

Vocabulary

Words and expressions: *rain hard, flat broke, salary rise, splitting headache, set up, fired, freeze to death, soaking wet, storm, borrow, get a loan, call in sick, order, I've had it!, change into something warm*

Comments

This activity focuses on the use of *will* for unplanned, spontaneous decisions. Although it does not really require language production, this game does provide a lot of useful input, and the quick pace actually reinforces this meaning of *will* here.

Language output

A: *It's your mother-in-law's birthday today.*
B: *Gosh, I almost forgot. I'll send her some flowers/I'll go to visit her then.*

Procedures

1 Before class, cut out one set of situation cards and one set of response cards for each group.

2 In class, write on the board a few situations similar to those on the situation cards. Ask students how they would respond spontaneously to each one of them. Elicit the responses and draw their attention to the meaning and use of *will*.

3 Divide the class into groups and hand out the material.

4 Playing the game:

  ▶ Players shuffle the situation cards and place them face down on the table. Then, they shuffle the response cards and deal them out evenly.

  ▶ The first player flips over the first situation card and reads it aloud. **Note:** The situation cards have been written the right way up and upside down so that everyone can see.

  ▶ The first player to call out an appropriate response to the situation gets rid of the corresponding response card that he or she holds. **Note:** There are always two possible responses to each situation, so players have to be quick.

  ▶ Players proceed in this way until someone has discarded all of his or her response cards and wins the game.

Situation cards

You have a splitting headache. / You have a splitting headache.	You've got a really bad cold. / You've got a really bad cold.	You're freezing to death. / You're freezing to death.	You arrive home soaking wet because of the storm. / You arrive home soaking wet because of the storm.
You've got a big salary rise. / You've got a big salary rise.	Your grandmother gives you £3,000 for your birthday. / Your grandmother gives you £3,000 for your birthday.	It's your mother-in-law's birthday today. / It's your mother-in-law's birthday today.	Your boss is in hospital. / Your boss is in hospital.
You're flat broke. / You're flat broke.	You want to set up your own business. / You want to set up your own business.	You've been fired. / You've been fired.	You hate your job. / You hate your job.
It is raining hard. / It is raining hard.	You've just fallen down in the middle of the street. / You've just fallen down in the middle of the street.	There is no food in the house. / There is no food in the house.	Your mother is coming over for dinner. / Your mother is coming over for dinner.

Response cards

I'll take a taxi.	I'll borrow some money from my father.	Great! I'll buy a new car.	I'll take an aspirin.
I'll go back home right now.	I'll probably get a loan from the bank.	I think I'll take a holiday in Tahiti.	I'll call in sick.
I'll go to the supermarket this afternoon.	I'll start looking for another job.	I'll send her some flowers.	I'll take a hot shower.
I'll order a pizza.	I've had it! I'll set up my own business.	I'll go to visit her.	I'll change into something warm.

5.1 Easy rider

Language focus

Mixed tenses

Level

Pre-intermediate

Type

Board game

Topic

Travelling

Interaction

Groups of three or four

Time

15–20 minutes

Material

Board, set of cards and dice (one per group), counters (one per student)

Vocabulary

Words and expressions: *like best about, a dream holiday, souvenirs, go abroad, oversleep, tourist guide, roulette*

Comments

This game offers learners an opportunity to review and practise mixed tenses (past, present and future), plus some modals, within a unified context and a fluency-building activity.

Language output

A: *Where did you spend your last holiday?*

B: *I went to the Greek Islands/I stayed at home/I visited my parents in the countryside.*

Procedures

1 Before class, cut out one set of cards for each group.

2 Strike up a conversation with the class on their last or next holiday to model the target language.

3 Divide the class into groups and hand out the material.

4 Playing the game:

> ❿ Players place their counters on the little aeroplane on the board. Then they shuffle the cards and pile them face down on the big suitcase on the board.

> ❿ Players take turns casting the dice and moving their counters accordingly.

> ❿ Whenever a player lands on a suitcase, the person to his or her right picks a card from the pile and asks him or her the question on it or reads out the events and instructions on the card. If it is a question, the first player answers, and the group may ask further questions or share their experiences on the topic. If it is an event plus instructions, the player follows them.

> ❿ The first player to get back to the little aeroplane, that is, to go round the world, wins the game.

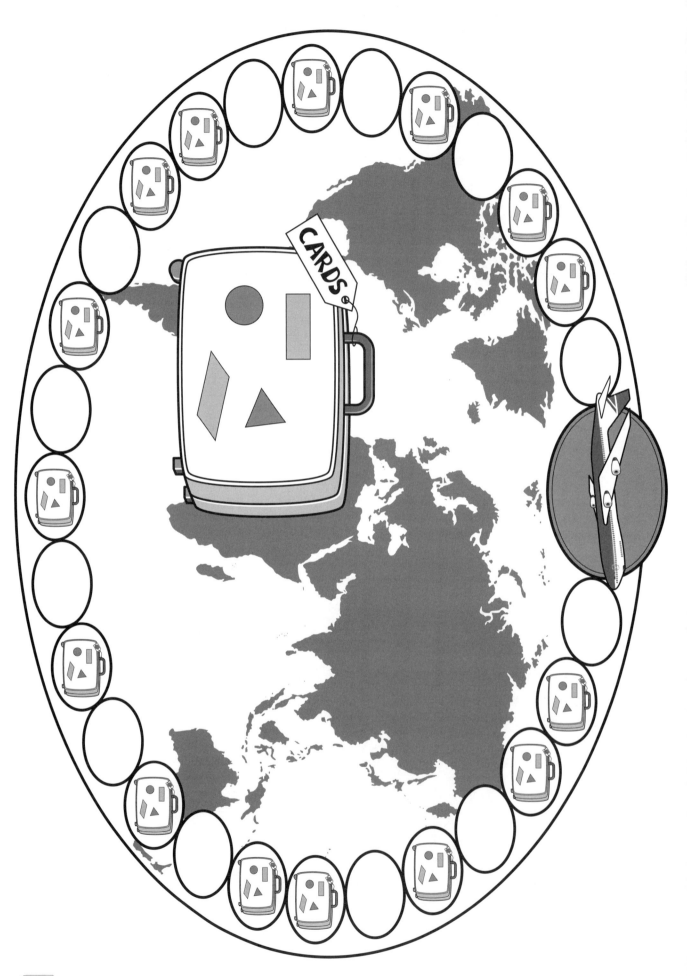

Cards

Where did you
spend your
last holiday?

Where do you
usually spend
your holidays?

Where are you
going on your
next holiday?

What did you like
best about your
last holiday?

What can a
tourist do in
your city?

Where would you
like to spend a
dream holiday?

What did you
buy on your
last trip?

What are good
souvenirs to buy
in your country?

What's your
favourite time
of year to go
on holiday?

Did you try
any special food
on your last trip?

What typical
dishes do tourists
usually enjoy in
your country?

When did you
last take
a holiday?

Where did you
stay on your
last trip?

Where do you
usually stay
when you travel?

How much is
a good hotel
in your city?

Cards

When are you going to take your next holiday?

What are three things you always carry on your trips?

What kind of clothes did you wear on your last holiday?

What's the best place for a tourist to visit in your country?

When are you planning to go abroad?

How did you travel on your last holiday?

You find out you still have some money left. Move on 3 squares.

You overslept and missed the train. Miss a turn.

Grandpa has sent you some money. Play again.

You can't find your wallet. Go back 2 squares.

You fall in love with a tourist guide... Move on 2 squares.

You've lost your passport and can't continue your trip. Miss a turn.

You win at roulette! Play again.

A friend gives you a lift. Play again.

The airport is closed. Miss a turn.

From *Games for Grammar Practice* © Cambridge University Press 2001 **PHOTOCOPIABLE**

6.1 Nothing's perfect! (I)

Language focus

First conditional

Level

Intermediate

Type

Simulation

Topic

Jobs

Interaction

Groups of three or six

Time

20 minutes

Material

Worksheet (one per group)

Vocabulary

Generated by students.

Comments

This activity focusing on the use of the first conditional is unique in that it is entirely generated by the students. The discussion it stimulates involves students' personal beliefs and preferences, in a context that they relate to.

Language output

A: *I have received these three job offers. Which one should I take?*

B: *If you take job A, you will get an excellent salary.*

C: *Yeah, but if you take that job, you will have to commute to work every day. Now, if you take job B, you will be able to walk to work.*

Procedures

1 Before class, take one copy of the worksheet for every group of three or six students. Cut each photocopy into three strips as indicated.

2 Divide the class into groups and give out one strip of the worksheet to each student (if working with groups of three) or pair (if working with groups of six). Just make sure that within each group, each student or pair will have a distinct strip.

3 Elicit from the class what they think a perfect/OK/lousy location, kind of work or pay would be. Tell them to write down their opinions under each heading, either individually or in pairs, according to the kind of job at the top of their strip. Circulate in the classroom and help them with any vocabulary they might need.

4 When they have finished, each student or pair tears up their strips into slips, along the broken lines.

5 Then, the whole group rearranges their slips by letter so as to obtain: six slips marked A, six slips marked B, and six other slips marked C.

6 Students change the titles of the jobs to A, B and C.

7 Each group then chooses one of its members to play the role of the person trying to decide which job to take. The student thus chosen begins interaction by explaining the situation and asking for advice, as shown in **Language output**. Students discuss the pros and cons of each one of the jobs using the first conditional, and try to come to a consensus as to the best choice for their classmate.

Variation

If your class does not relate to the topic, use *Nothing's perfect! (II)*, which is based on holidays. Follow the same procedures.

A Lousy Job

Location	C
Kind of work	C
Pay	A
Working hours	A
Prospects	B
Holiday and benefits	B

An OK Job

Location	B
Kind of work	B
Pay	C
Working hours	C
Prospects	A
Holiday and benefits	A

A Perfect Job

Location	A
Kind of work	A
Pay	B
Working hours	B
Prospects	C
Holiday and benefits	C

A Lousy Holiday

C
Destination

A
Time of year

B
Travel companion

B
Type of accommodation

C
Daytime activities

A
Nightlife

An OK Holiday

B
Destination

C
Time of year

A
Travel companion

A
Type of accommodation

B
Daytime activities

C
Nightlife

A Perfect Holiday

A
Destination

B
Time of year

C
Travel companion

C
Type of accommodation

A
Daytime activities

B
Nightlife

6.2 Watch your step!

Language focus

Second conditional

Level

Intermediate

Type

Snakes and ladders

Topic

Unusual behaviour

Interaction

Groups of two or six

Time

20 minutes

Material

Board and dice (one per group), counters (one per student)

Vocabulary

Words and expressions: *deliberately, ant hill, charity, fast (verb), lamp post, bunch of flowers, scream, tear up*

Comments

This board game invites learners to imagine the reasons for very unusual or even nonsensical behaviour to stimulate the use of second conditionals to talk about very unlikely situations. It provides practice and sheer fun.

Language output

A: *Would you ever shave your head?*

B: *Yes, I would (shave my head) if I were paid a lot of money to do that.*

or

B: *No, I wouldn't (shave my head), because if I did/shaved my head, I would/might lose my job.*

Procedures

1 Write a skeleton on the board for the dialogue in ***Language output***. Model the language by playing A's part and eliciting several responses from your class. Draw their attention to the verb forms and modals used.

2 Divide the class into groups and hand out the material.

3 Playing the game:

- ▶ Players place their counters at START.
- ▶ They take turns rolling the dice and moving their counters accordingly.
- ▶ Whenever a player lands on a square with a question in it, some other player will direct a *Would you ever …?* question to him or her, and they interact as shown in ***Language output***.
- ▶ If the answer is correct and considered plausible by the group, the player moves forward three squares; otherwise, he or she will move back one square.
- ▶ Whenever a player lands on a footprint, he or she must follow the path, moving either up or down all the way to the end.
- ▶ The first player to get to (but not beyond) the FINISH point wins the game.

Variation

If you want learners to really tap into their imagination and make the game even more humorous, have them answer affirmatively to all the questions.

finish

start

Would you ever...

1	eat five dozen bananas in a day?
3	wear a winter coat in the summer?
5	go out with someone you really didn't like?
7	buy yourself a lion?
10	buy yourself a lion?
14	drink a litre of whisky?
17	deliberately sit on an ant hill?
20	give all your money to charity?
21	dress up as a person of the opposite sex?
23	spend a month on a desert island?
25	go swimming with your clothes on?
27	fast for seven days?
29	go without speaking to anyone for a week?
31	crash your car into a lamp post?
32	cross the street without looking?
34	move to Alaska?
36	send yourself a bunch of flowers?
39	scream for half an hour without a break?
40	wear sunglasses at night?
42	deliberately tear up money?
43	shave your head?

6.3 Pick my good deed

Language focus

Third conditional

Level

Upper-intermediate or advanced

Type

Board game

Topic

Justifying actions

Interaction

Groups of two or six

Time

15–20 minutes

Material

Board, dice, and set of cards (one per group), counters (one per student)

Vocabulary

Words and expressions: *log cabin, can afford, pneumonia, ball (dance), have the heart to, homework assignment, bad mark, make it to (a place), be worn out*

Comments

This game provides plenty of situations that stimulate the use of third conditionals. Even though it has been devised so as to keep the condition statement constant while cueing learners to vary only the expression of consequence, it can be easily adapted for variation in both parts of the conditional structure.

Language output

A: *Jean was so depressed. She had no company for the weekend.*

B: *Oh, if I'd known (she had no company), I'd / I would have invited her out to a movie.*

Procedures

1 Using some of the situations on the cards, elicit and model the language shown in **Language output**. Make sure you draw your learners' attention to the meaning of this structure as well as to the verb forms and modals used.

2 Divide the class into groups and hand out the material.

3 Set the context by telling your class: *You are all very nice people and love to help others. Whenever you hear that someone has had a problem, you express how sorry you are for not having been able to help, and say what you would have done to help if only you'd known!*

4 Playing the game:

▶ Players place their counters on the four START corners of the board. Then, they shuffle the cards and pile them face down in the centre of the board.

▶ Players take turns casting the dice and moving their counters accordingly. Whenever a player lands on a square with a 'saintly-looking face' in it, the person to his or her left picks a card and reads out the situation. The player then responds as shown in **Language output**.
Note: Encourage peer monitoring to ensure accuracy. If the player lands in a square that has a hand in it, he or she must move forward or backward as indicated.

▶ The first player to get to (but not beyond) the FINISH square wins the game.

Note on class size

If students are playing in groups of five or six, they can share the START corners on the board.

Variation

If you want your students to practise varying both parts of the conditional structure, elicit several possibilities when you introduce the activity, e.g.

A: *Jean was so depressed. She had no company for the weekend.*

B: *Yeah, I know. If it hadn't rained all weekend, I'd have invited her out for a picnic.*
If I hadn't had to work all weekend, I'd have taken her out to dinner.
If I had had her phone number, I'd have called and asked her out to a movie.

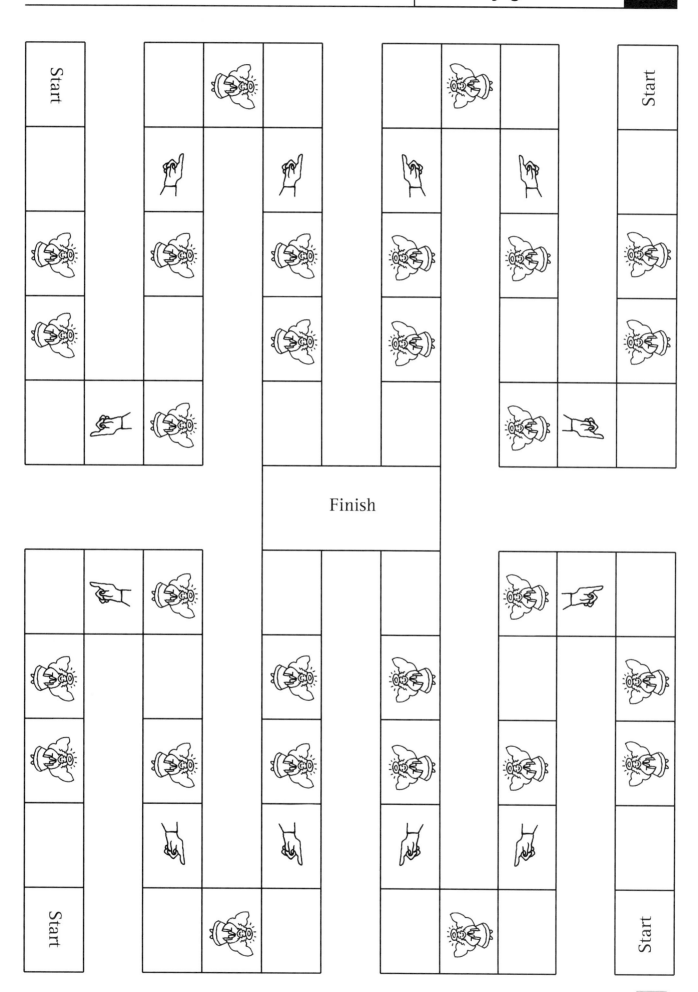

Start

Finish

Start

Start

Start

Cards

Your cousin Jody was in hospital last week, and you didn't even go to visit her.	How come you let Ann walk home all by herself after your party last night?	Joe said he went to visit you last Sunday, but you weren't at home.	Jane is very upset with you. You didn't invite her for the weekend in your log cabin in the mountains.
Poor Bill couldn't go to the concert last week because he couldn't afford a ticket.	Your brother stayed at home all weekend because his car was in the garage.	Jean was so depressed. She had no company for the weekend.	Douglas went out for lunch without an umbrella. Now he is in bed with pneumonia.
Mary got into a lot of trouble because she couldn't finish typing the reports for the meeting.	Ray and Meg didn't go out to celebrate their anniversary. They couldn't get a baby-sitter for their four kids.	Greg didn't go home for Thanksgiving because he didn't have enough money for the plane ticket.	Amy was very upset. None of her friends remembered her birthday.
Kathy broke her leg and couldn't drive. That's why she didn't come to class today.	Kim didn't take any pictures on her last holiday. She didn't have a good camera, poor thing!	Poor Gordon has been wearing the same shirt all week. His washing machine is not working.	Keith invited 10 friends for dinner last night, but he'd never cooked for so many people. He was desperate!
Because she didn't have anything nice to wear, Robin couldn't go to the ball last Friday.	Betty couldn't go away for the weekend, because she didn't have the heart to leave her five cats alone for so long.	Just because he didn't do his homework assignment, Brian got a bad mark.	Charles didn't make it to your party last night because he didn't know how to get to your house.
Your mother was definitely upset. She didn't hear a word from you during your whole holiday.	You know that dictionary you borrowed? The teacher needed it so badly, she had to go out and buy another one.	Harold missed his plane because there was nobody to take him to the airport.	Ray spent the whole weekend painting his new apartment. No wonder he was worn out on Monday!

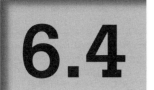

6.4 The wish race

Language focus

Wish constructions

Level

Intermediate or
upper-intermediate

Type

Grid game

Topic

Regrets and complaints

Interaction

Groups of two to four

Time

15–20 minutes

Material

Grid (one per group),
counters (one per student)

Vocabulary

Words and expressions: *stuff, in-laws, without notice, gallon, oversleep, instant noodles, hangover, run out of*

Comments

The objective here is to provide open-ended, but still controlled, practice with various sorts of *wish* constructions. The game focuses on meaning and form in that it requires learners to produce forms (simple, perfect and/or continuous) that are appropriate for the situation given.

Language output

I wish my mother were not so nosy!
hadn't opened my mail.
would learn to respect my privacy.

Procedures

1 On the board, write down a few situations that are similar to those on the grid. Elicit responses to the situations with *wish* constructions. Draw students' attention to the relation between the verb forms and the meaning they express.

2 Divide the class into groups and hand out the material.

3 Playing the game:

▶ Players place their counters at A to D on the left-hand side of the grid. Their objective is to be the first to reach the corresponding end points on the opposite side of the grid.

▶ Players may move horizontally or vertically across the grid, one circle at a time, provided they can come up with a *wish* sentence that is both correct and appropriate for the situation in the target circle. **Note:** You may want to encourage your learners to elaborate on their statements, e.g. *I wish my mother hadn't opened my mail. I hate having to fight with her for my right to privacy!*

▶ If a player wants to move into a circle that has already been occupied by another player, he or she must produce a different 'wish' sentence.

▶ The first player to reach his or her end circle wins the game.

Variation

If you want to restrict the game to a single category of *wish* construction, just make sure the situations in the circles will generate the same kind of construction.

C

You ran out of petrol on the way to the airport and missed the plane.

You crashed your mother's car last night.

Your boyfriend/girlfriend is always too busy to go out with you.

You got drunk last night and now you've got a terrible hangover.

A

D

You live on instant noodles because you can't cook.

You didn't pass your last English test.

It's raining hard, but your umbrella is at home.

You overslept and arrived late for a very important meeting this morning.

B

A

Your mother opened a letter addressed to you.

You'll have to work this Saturday.

You had a gallon of ice-cream this afternoon and now you've got an upset stomach.

You can't find a job because you are not experienced enough.

C

B

Your in-laws have just arrived for a 10-day visit without notice.

Your apartment is too small for all your stuff.

You had a fight with your boss and he fired you.

You'd give anything to be 10 centimetres taller.

D

7.1 Who's got my message?

Language focus

Reported speech

Level

Intermediate

Type

Card game

Topic

Telephone messages

Interaction

Groups of three to five

Time

15–20 minutes

Material

Two sets of cards per group

Vocabulary

Words and expressions: *insurance company, personnel, physiotherapist, overdrawn, reschedule, make it to (a place), break down*

Comments

This card game provides contextualized and interactive practice with the reported speech of statements, questions and requests, as used in a real life situation: that of giving messages. Learners are given the contents of telephone messages and asked to transform them into full reported speech constructions.

Language output

A: *Have you got any message for me from my lawyer?*

B: *Yes. She said that your documents were/are ready, and asked/wants you to come and sign them tomorrow.*

or

B: *Sorry. Maybe someone else.*

Procedures

1 Before class, cut out one set of sender cards and one set of message cards for each group.

2 In class, write on the board a few messages similar to those on the cards. Elicit and model the language as shown in *Language output*. **Note:** You may want to stick to the verb agreement principle or show that this principle is, in fact, overridden by other factors in speech, e.g. *She said that your documents **are** ready …* rather than … **were** ready … .

3 Divide the class into groups and hand out the material.

4 Set the situation by telling your class: *The secretaries were absent from work today, so everybody had to take turns taking down messages for everyone else. However, the messages got mixed up. Find your messages.*

5 Playing the game:

- Players shuffle and deal out both sets of cards and check for any sender and message matches. If there are any, they set them aside.
- Players take turns trying to guess who has the message cards that match the sender cards that they hold. Each player will do that by choosing someone that they think has the target message card, and initiating the conversation in *Language output* with that person. If the answer is affirmative, the message is delivered and the player collects the target message card; otherwise, the player only gets a negative answer.
- The first player to collect all of his or her message cards wins the game.

Variation

If you want to focus on reporting either statements, or questions or requests alone, devise your own message cards accordingly.

Note on class size

When playing in groups of five, remove one of the sender cards from the pack, along with the corresponding message card, so that all the players will get the same number of cards.

Sender cards

from your
sisters

from your
lawyer

from the bank

from your
dentist

from Jennifer

from your
English teacher

from your
secretary

from your
parents

from your
cousin Paul

from the
insurance
company

from the library

from the
repair shop

from personnel

from your
physiotherapist

from your
grandma

from your kids

Message cards

FROM:
sisters

MESSAGE:
Call as soon as possible. Will be at Aunt Agatha's.

FROM:
lawyer

MESSAGE:
Documents are ready. Come and sign them tomorrow.

FROM:
bank

MESSAGE:
Account is overdrawn. Make a deposit urgently.

FROM:
dentist

MESSAGE:
Appointment cancelled. Call this afternoon to reschedule it.

FROM:
Jennifer

MESSAGE:
Going to make special lasagna tomorrow. Bring some wine.

FROM:
teacher

MESSAGE:
Car has broken down. Can't make it to class today. Will call tomorrow to set replacement class.

FROM:
secretary

MESSAGE:
In bed with the flu. Won't come the rest of the week.

FROM:
parents

MESSAGE:
Arriving tomorrow morning. Pick them up at the airport at 6 a.m.

FROM:
Paul

MESSAGE:
Forgot to pay phone bill. Call back before 6:30. Will be at the office.

FROM:
insurance company

MESSAGE:
Documents authorizing the repairs are ready. Can take car to any garage.

FROM:
library

MESSAGE:
Have got the book you wanted. Will keep it for two days.

FROM:
repair shop

MESSAGE:
Haven't fixed the CD player yet. Will call when it is ready.

FROM:
personnel

MESSAGE:
Need a recent photo. Bring it in by the end of the week.

FROM:
physiotherapist

MESSAGE:
Can schedule extra session the day after tomorrow. Call and confirm with secretary.

FROM:
grandmother

MESSAGE:
Needs help with new TV. Please stop by tomorrow morning.

FROM:
kids

MESSAGE:
Want to spend the night at David's. Call to say it's OK.

8.1 Crazy cans

Language focus

Can for ability

Level

Elementary

Type

Crazy eights

Topic

Abilities

Interaction

Groups of three to four

Time

10–15 minutes

Material

One set of cards per group

Vocabulary

Words and expressions: *mother, father, best friend, teacher, Mexican, Spanish, man, woman, people, birds, kangaroo, flea, monkey, squirrel, penguin, duck, cat, owl, child, parrot, aeroplane, Superman, gun, knife, computer, calculator, turtle, tree, Porsche, cheetah*

Comments

Based on Crazy eights (commercially known as UNO), this game gets players to think what the pairs of items on the cards have in common in terms of skills or abilities (see **Possible answers** on page 114), and express that using *can*. They must also learn to use strategy to win, but the wild cards may spin the whole thing around!

Language output

A: *What can a bird and Superman do?*

B: *Both can fly.*

Procedures

1 Before class, cut out one set of cards for each group.

2 In class, write a few pairs of items similar to those on the cards, and model the target language as shown in **Language output**.

3 Divide the class into groups and hand out the material.

4 Playing the game:

▶ Players shuffle the cards and deal them out as shown below. The remaining cards are piled face down in the middle.

Number of players	3	4	5
Cards per player	5	4	3
Cards in the pile	5	4	5

▶ The youngest in the group chooses one of his or her cards, lays it on the table, and directs a question to the player on his or her right, as shown in **Language output**.

▶ If the respondent gives an answer that is accepted by the group, then he or she wins the right to pick one of his or her cards, lay it down and direct a question to the next player. If the answer is not accepted, then he or she is not allowed to lay down any of his or her cards, but the next player is, and the game proceeds from there.

▶ The REVERSE, SKIP, BUY ONE, BUY TWO, and CHOOSE PLAYER cards can be used by any player who holds them to delay opponents at any point during the game. The player just says out loud *SKIP!*, *REVERSE!*, etc. and the group must follow the order (see below).

▶ The first player to get rid of all of his or her cards wins the game.

Note on game rules

Explain to your students the meanings of the wild cards, which are the following:

▶ REVERSE = the game changes direction

▶ SKIP = the player to the right of the one holding this card misses a turn

▶ BUY ONE and BUY TWO = the next player must buy one or two cards from the pile

▶ CHOOSE PLAYER = the player holding this card may choose the next player to have the right to lay down a card and ask a question

your mother & your father	a kangaroo & a flea	an aeroplane & Superman	REVERSE
your best friend & you	a monkey & a squirrel	a gun & a knife	SKIP
your teacher & you	a penguin & a duck	a computer & a calculator	BUY ONE
a Mexican man & a Spanish woman	a cat & an owl	a turtle & a tree	BUY TWO
people & birds	a child & a parrot	a Porsche & a cheetah	CHOOSE PLAYER

8.2 Let's go together

Language focus

Like v. *would like*

Level

Elementary

Type

Find someone who

Topic

Invitations

Interaction

Mixer/mingle activity

Time

10–20 minutes

Material

Cards (one per student)

Vocabulary

Kinds of food and entertainment. Some of the vocabulary in the material may be new to elementary learners, but it is not intended for production. Just make sure they can extract from the ads the information they will need to carry out their task.

Comments

Here, learners are given a task – to invite someone out – and go around the classroom interacting with peers in order to accomplish it. The material offers plenty of input and variety, plus the context for this highly interactive activity involving the use of *like* v. *would like*.

Language output

A: *Do you like Middle-Eastern food?*
B: *Well, not really.*
A: *Oh, OK, maybe someone else.*

or

A: *Do you like Middle-Eastern food?*
B: *Oh, yes, I do.*
A: *Great! Would you like to go to Ali's Restaurant with me?*
B: *Sure. I'd love to. When?*
A: *How about tonight, at 8?*
B: *Sounds fine. See you then.*

Procedures

1 Before class, cut out the cards, one for every student.

2 In class, model the interaction above using the names of real places or events in town. While modelling, encourage students to practise declining an invitation as well.

3 Hand out the cards.

4 Set the context by telling your class: *You want to go to the place on your card, but you also want company. Invite your classmates to go with you. Every time someone accepts, write his or her name on the card, plus the date and time.*

5 Doing the activity:

▶ Students move around talking to their classmates. They may accept as many invitations as they wish, provided they are not for the same date and time!

▶ Stop the activity when you feel they have had enough practice. Find out from the class which were the most popular places or outings.

Note on class size

If your class has more than 18 students, split it into two or three groups and have students interact within their groups.

Variation

You may choose to concentrate on a single type of outing, e.g. eating out, in which case you should divide the class into groups of six so that each student may have a different card. Students will then interact within their groups.

Chez Loulou

An Authentic French Bistro

Call for reservations
275-3992

Reservations _____

_____

_____

Gerta's All Natural

*Vegetarian food
that tastes good*

Lunch and Dinner   Mon – Sun

Reservations _____

_____

_____

The Hamburger Land

Special double burger: £1.50
Cheeseburger: £1.99
French Fries: 50p

Open 24 hours

Reservations _____

_____

_____

ALI'S RESTAURANT

Best Middle-Eastern
food in town

Open
11 a.m.–11 p.m.

Reservations _____

_____

_____

The Chinese Delight

All you can
eat for £5 !!!

Don't miss our fantastic spring rolls

Reservations _____

_____

_____

Frozen Dreams

The real Italian ice-cream

Reservations _____

_____

_____

A concert for classical music lovers

Vivaldi
The Four Seasions
The Kinnelon Chamber Orchestra

Fridays: 8 p.m. Sunday: 6 p.m.

Tickets

_____

_____

Jazz Heaven

Feel like you are in the heart of fantastic New Orleans

Shows: 9 and 11 p.m.
Tuesday to Saturday

Tickets

_____

_____

COUNTRY NIGHT

Five Different Bands

It's fun

It's wild

Every Friday and Saturday at *The Mill*

Tickets

_____

_____

A Night in Spain

Flamenco Dance
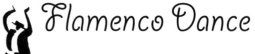

Romance and fun all night long

Shows: Tue to Sun 10 pm

Tickets

_____

_____

Erik Clark

**and his romantic piano
in a recital to remember**

Holywell Music Room

Thursday, Friday and Saturday at 7:30 pm

Tickets

_____

_____

Ted Mort and the super mob

The best rock of all times

This week only
Friday, Saturday and Sunday
at 9: 30 pm

Tickets

_____

_____

From *Games for Grammar Practice* © Cambridge University Press 2001 **PHOTOCOPIABLE**

THE HAND OF DEATH

The spookiest horror film ever made.

The Everyman Theatre
Shows: daily at midnight

Tickets

_____

_____

_____

Museum of Modern Art

The great artists of the 90s

Hours: Mon–Sat 10 am to 5 pm

Tickets

_____

_____

_____

Miss Saigon
The Most Acclaimed Musical of the Year

Royal Festival House
Shows: Mon – Sat at 8 pm
Sun at 2 and 7 pm.

Tickets

_____

_____

_____

The Bulls X The Bears

Playing in the semi-finals

Friday at _Chicago Arena_ 8:30 pm

Tickets

_____

_____

_____

The Nutcracker
San Francisco Ballet Company

The Grand National Theatre
Wed–Sat at 8:00 pm
Sun at 10:00 am

Tickets

_____

_____

_____

The Puppy Show
sponsored by the International Kennel Club

Great entertainment for dog lovers

Hours: Friday – Sunday
9:00 am – 6:00 pm

Tickets

_____

_____

_____

8.3 Spinning ideas

Language focus

Modals (simple)

Level

Pre-intermediate

Type

Scattergories

Topic

Constraints and possibilities

Interaction

Teams of two to four

Time

15–20 minutes

Material

Board and dice
(one for every two teams)

Vocabulary

Modals: *can, can't, should, shouldn't, have to, don't have to*

Comments

Based on a game commercially known as Scattergories, this game is meant for intensive practice with modals to express possibility, necessity, obligation and advice. The game requires that learners focus on the meaning of the modals and situations drawn on the dice, and produce sentences that are correct, meaningful and appropriate, but at the same time original, in order to win the game.

Language output

When you are on holiday you don't usually have to worry about the time.
If you are in a foreign country, you should try to learn simple words and phrases in the local language.

Procedures

1 List the modals and write the following on the board:
When you are at work, … .
Then elicit from the class various endings for this sentence using the modals listed. Draw their attention to meaning, form and appropriateness.

2 Divide the class into teams, pair off teams, and hand out the material.

3 Playing the game:

▶ Every two teams should appoint one player to keep the score and another player to time the teams' work.

▶ Team A casts the dice: once to set the situation according to the circle on the left side of the board, and once to set the modal in accordance with the circle on the right.

▶ Then both teams have, let's say, one or two minutes to write down as many sentences containing the modal as they can, for the situation drawn.

▶ When the time is up, the teams take turns reading out the sentences produced. They score one point for every meaningful and appropriate sentence, and two points for every such sentence that is also original, i.e. not thought up by their opponents.

▶ The two teams take turns proceeding in this way until the end of the game, which is determined by the teacher. They add up their scores, and the team with the highest score wins the game.

Variation

You may want to replace the situations on the board with the following, which are more specific:

▶ You are trying to save money
▶ You are unemployed
▶ You are moving to a foreign country
▶ You are soon to be married
▶ You are visiting your in-laws for the first time
▶ You badly want to lose some weight

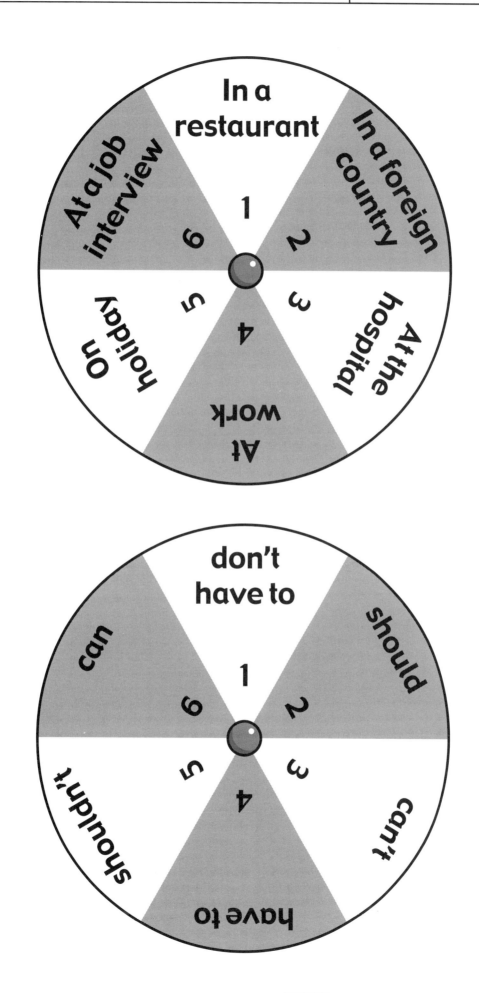

8.4 Tough luck!

Vocabulary

Modals: *may, might, could, must, can't, couldn't*

Words and expressions: *be turned down, fail, gifted, no matter what, show up, broken-hearted, house-warming party, call off, be born with a silver spoon in one's mouth*

Comments

This game gives each pair of learners two ends of a situation involving two characters, John and Mary, and challenges them to work out what may have happened in the middle, to practise the perfect and perfect continuous forms of *may, might, could, must, can't* and *couldn't*. The fast-moving pace requires that learners exercise quick and imaginative thinking to come up with arguments to justify their own hypotheses and counter their opponent's.

Language output

Situation: John invited Mary over for dinner last night. Mary went over, but no one answered the door.

A: *John might have fallen asleep while waiting for Mary to show up.*

B: *No, he couldn't have fallen asleep while waiting for her. He's madly in love with her and was so anxious to see her! He must have gone out on an emergency call. He's a doctor, remember?*

A: *No, that couldn't have been the case. He wouldn't have accepted being on call if he had been planning to spend the evening with her. The intercom must have been broken. …*

Procedures

1 Before class, cut out one set of cards for every pair of students and place the sets in bags or envelopes.

2 On the board, write down a situation whose outcome is totally unexpected, preferably with the same format as that shown on the cards. Then, list the modals on the board. Elicit from the class what might have happened. For every hypothesis the class presents, work out a counterargument, justify it, and present a new hypothesis along with a justification for the class to argue against. Do this several times until the class has grasped the chain: hypothesis – counterargument and justification – new hypothesis and justification, and so on. Also, make sure students understand the meaning of the modals and are able to use them correctly.

3 Pair off students and hand out the bags or envelopes.

4 Playing the game:

 ▶ The first player draws a card from the bag or envelope, reads out the situation, and presents the first hypothesis. His or her opponent must then come up with a counterargument, justification and a new hypothesis. They go on like this until one of them is left with no more arguments and gives up. The opponent then wins the situation card. **Note:** Players may make up any facts about John and Mary to justify their arguments.

 ▶ When you think the students have played enough, stop the game and have players count their cards. Whoever has the largest number of cards wins the game.

Note on class size and material

When working with a large class, hand out sets of the cards on the first page to half of the pairs in class, and sets of the cards on the second page to the other half of pairs. When pairs with different sets have used up all their cards, have them swap their sets. This should save you time and work.

John was the most experienced candidate.	**?**	He was turned down for the job.
Mary studied like crazy for the exam.	**?**	She failed the exam.
John invited Mary over for dinner last night.	**?**	Mary went over, but no one answered the door.
Mary was away from home on holiday.	**?**	She got an incredibly high telephone bill.
John was a gifted piano player.	**?**	He became an engineer.
Mary said she would come to the party no matter what.	**?**	She didn't show up at all.

Mary was planning to get married next month.	**?**	Now she is broken-hearted.
Mary planned a great house-warming party.	**?**	The party was called off at the last minute.
John left home four hours before his plane was supposed to take off.	**?**	He ended up missing the flight.
John was born with a silver spoon in his mouth.	**?**	Now he can't pay for his beer.
Mary was very excited about her trip to Greece.	**?**	She has decided to stay at home instead.
John moved to his own apartment less than a month ago.	**?**	He is back in his mother's home.

9.1 Something in common

Language focus

Simple present and past passive

Level

Elementary and intermediate

Type

Trivia pursuit

Topic

World knowledge

Interaction

Teams of two or three

Time

15–20 minutes

Material

Set of cards (one per group)

Vocabulary

Nouns: *forks, coins, polar bears, penguins, bottle opener, corkscrew, shower cap, credit card, tennis, squash, shoes, socks, paints, brushes, newspapers, magazines, coffee, cotton, presents, greeting cards, glass, cement, stamps, airletters*

Comments

This game provides practice with the simple present passive while challenging learners to think of what the pairs of items have in common (see ***Possible answers*** on page 114). It focuses on accuracy of form, encourages cooperation within teams, and is sheer fun to play.

Language output

Team A: *What do glass and cement have in common?*
Team B: *Glass and cement / Both are made from sand.*

Procedures

1 Before class, cut out one set of cards for every two teams and place the sets in bags or envelopes.

2 On the board, write down a few pairs of items similar to those on the cards, and elicit what the items have in common. With each pair of items, model and monitor the target language.

3 Divide the class into teams of two or three, pair off teams, and hand out the bags or envelopes.

4 Playing the game:

▶ Every two teams must appoint one player to time the game and keep the score.

▶ Team A draws a card from the bag or envelope and challenges Team B with *What do … and … have in common?* Team B has some (pre-established) time to discuss among themselves and produce an answer using the target language. If it is accepted by everyone in terms of meaning and form, Team B collects the card. Otherwise, Team A gets the chance to find a good answer and collect the card themselves.

▶ Teams take turns proceeding in this way until all the cards have been used. The team with the largest number of cards wins the game.

Variations

▶ You can use the same procedures to practise simple past passive with pairs of items such as those suggested below. Just make sure you tailor the items to your students' age and culture by including facts about popular music, entertainment, local history, and so on. Remember: our aim is to get learners to practise the target language; the challenge is there to make the game more interesting, not to test their world knowledge!

Pyramids and sphinxes		built by the Ancient Egyptians.
Jurassic Park and *E.T.*	were	directed by Spielberg.
Yellow Submarine and *Yesterday*		recorded by the Beatles.

▶ You may also want to encourage the use of *Both … and / Neither … nor* in the answers, in both versions of the game.

Forks **Coins**	**Tennis** **Squash**	**Coffee** **Cotton**
Polar bears **Penguins**	**Shoes** **Socks**	**Presents** **Greeting cards**
Bottle opener **Corkscrew**	**Paints** **Brushes**	**Glass** **Cement**
Shower cap **Credit card**	**Newspapers** **Magazines**	**Stamps** **Airletters**

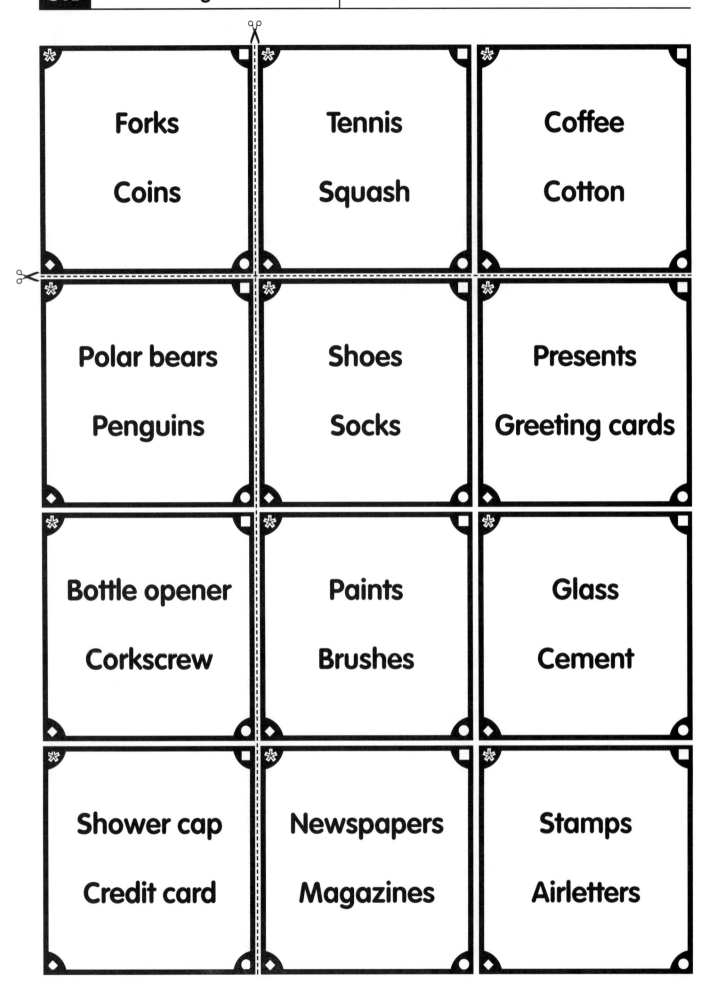

9.2 Grown-ups!

Language focus

Passive + infinitive

Level

Intermediate to advanced

Type

Discussion

Topic

Growing-up experiences

Interaction

Groups of three or four

Time

20 minutes

Material

Worksheets (one per student), set of slips (one per group)

Vocabulary

Verbs: *asked, told, taught, advised, brought up, encouraged, expected, warned, allowed, forbidden, supposed, forced*

Comments

This fluency-building activity invites learners to share and discuss their growing-up experiences while practising passives followed by infinitives, as in *I wasn't allowed to smoke*. Its design guarantees that everyone will have an equal opportunity to prepare for and initiate discussion. In addition to exposing learners to a variety of verbs used in this construction and focusing on its meaning, it is great for promoting class rapport.

Language output

A: *When I was a teenager, I was asked to pay for part of our household expenses.*
B: *I wasn't asked to pay for any expenses, but I was expected to share in the household chores.*

Procedures

1 Before class, take copies of the worksheet, one for every student. Then, cut off the grid at the bottom of the worksheets, and reserve one for every group. Finally, cut the grids into slips and put them into bags or envelopes, again one bag or envelope for every group. Such slips are meant to ensure that all students can participate equally in the activity.

2 On the board, write down a few of the verbs from the worksheet and model the target language. Elicit from the class statements about their personal growing-up experiences, and write them on the board as well. Draw their attention to the target structure. Then, finalize with a brief discussion as to how they felt and whether they think their parents/teachers were right.

3 Divide the class into groups and hand out the material.

4 Doing the activity:

▶ Individually, students fill out the chart on the worksheet by writing one sentence about themselves with each one of the verbs given.

▶ In each group, students will decide who will be A, B, C and D, and write their names next to the corresponding letters just below the chart.

▶ The group picks a slip from the bag or envelope. If, for example, the slip reads B2, then student B reads out his or her sentence number 2, which must contain the verb *told to*. The others then contribute with their own experiences, using the same verb. Finally, they discuss whether they think their parents/teachers, etc. were right, and whether they would do the same with their children/students, etc.

When I was ... I was(n't) ... (not) to ...
1   asked
2   told
3   taught
4   advised
5   brought up
6   encouraged
7   expected
8   warned
9   allowed
10   forbidden
11   supposed
12   forced

A........................ **B**........................ **C**........................ **D**........................
   (name)   *(name)*   *(name)*   *(name)*

A1	B2	C3	D4
A5	B6	C7	D8
A9	B10	C11	D12

9.3 Round the clock

Language focus

Causative with *have*

Level

Intermediate to advanced

Type

Role play

Topic

Errands and services

Interaction

Groups of two to four

Time

20 minutes

Material

Board, set of cards, and coins (one per group), counters (one per student)

Vocabulary

Places: *cleaner's, garage, shoe repair shop, photo shop, hair stylist, photocopy shop, translation bureau (certified translations), dressmaker/tailor (alterations), optician (eye care), locksmith, electronics repair shop, chemist*

Words and expressions: *old-fashioned, sole, polishing, spill, ink stain, sleeve, hay fever, prescription, freelancer, tight, insist on, school transcript*

Comments

In this task-oriented activity, learners receive errands to run. They go to various places and engage in full conversations to accomplish their tasks, using the causative form with *have*. The target structure is thus contextualized and practised communicatively.

Language output

A: *Good morning.*
B: *Good morning. Can I help you?*
A: *Yes, I'd like to have these shoes repaired, and I want to have them polished too.*
B: *Yes, sir. They should be ready on Monday.*
A: *Monday! Can't I have them ready before that? You see, they're my favourite …*
B: *Well, let's see … Would this Thursday be OK?*
A: *Sure, much better. Should I pay you now?*
B: *Oh, no. Only when you come to pick them up on Thursday.*
A: *Fine, then. Thanks a lot. See you on Thursday.*
B: *See you. Have a nice day.*

Procedures

1 Divide the class into groups and hand out the material.

2 Explain to your students that they will be getting things done at each one of the places on the board. Elicit the kind of conversation that usually takes place in such situations and demonstrate the game a couple of times by playing the role of student A, and then of student B.

3 Playing the game:

▶ Players shuffle the cards, deal them out evenly, and place their counters at START on the board.

▶ The first player tosses the coin and moves his or her counter clockwise, one square for heads, and two squares for tails. If it lands on a place where he or she can run one of the errands on his or her cards, the player begins interaction with the person to his or her right. When they have finished, the first player discards the errand he or she has just run. Otherwise, no interaction takes place.

▶ Players take turns proceeding in this way until everyone has moved round the clock once.

▶ Players count the cards they are still holding. Whoever has the smallest number of cards, i.e. has run the largest number of errands, wins the game.

Cards

You need 100 copies of the new price list – both sides. Note: your boss wants them on his desk by the end of the afternoon.	Your hair is definitely too long and old-fashioned. You want something more modern and not too short.	You and your best friend have just got back from a holiday in Thailand, where you took dozens of pictures. You want two copies of each picture: one for you and one for your friend.
There is a big hole in the sole of your favourite and most comfortable shoes. They also need polishing. Why not try that new shoe repair shop down the street?	Your car is making a strange noise, and it is not as economical as it once was. Nick is supposed to be a fantastic mechanic and his prices are not too bad.	Your nephew has spilled ice-cream all over your overcoat. Better have a professional take care of it. Maybe they can do something about that old ink stain on the sleeve, too.
Spring has finally come, and so has your hay fever. Your doctor wants you to try a stronger prescription. You need it before you go away on business tomorrow evening.	Your answering machine is not recording the messages. Because you are a freelancer, you really depend on it for contacts and new clients.	Your two cousins are coming to spend a week at your place. You'll be busy working most of the time, so they need to have a copy of the front door key.
You have been having problems driving in the evening. You think you might need new glasses. Some friends have told you about Best Vision. They are said to be very competent.	The trousers your sister gave you for Christmas are a bit tight and way too long. They do a good job at Perfect Fit, even though you have to insist on fast service.	You are applying for a university course in Australia. They insist on having a certified translation of your school transcripts and diplomas.

10.1 Making friends

Language focus

Wh- questions with present simple

Level

Beginner or elementary

Type

Find someone who

Topic

Personal information

Interaction

Mixer/mingle activity

Time

10–20 minutes

Material

Worksheet (one per student)

Vocabulary

Wh- words: *what, when, how many, where, how, how old*

Verbs: *be, have, live, come*

Nouns and adjectives: *phone number, last name, birthday, favourite, kind (noun), food, colour, toothbrush, number, brothers, sisters, class, parents*

Comments

You may use this activity to review wh- questions with *be* and other verbs in the present simple, and/or to help your learners to become better acquainted with one another. It gives basic learners an opportunity to interact and socialize with a large number of peers in English despite their limited scope of communication.

Language output

A: *When is your birthday?*

B: *My birthday is on June 5th.*

A: *Really? My birthday is in June too! / Oh, my birthday is in April.*

Procedures

1 Hand out the worksheets and explain the objective of the activity by saying: *You must find classmates who have things in common with you, that is, who do or have something the same as you.*

2 Go over each one of the boxes and elicit the questions students would have to ask to find out who they have things in common with, e.g. *When's your birthday? / What colour is your toothbrush? / What's your favourite food? / How old are your parents? / Where do you live? / How many brothers and sisters have you got? / What's your last name? / How do you come to class? / What's your phone number?*

3 Demonstrate the dialogue in ***Language output*** to show the kind of language they may use. Repeat this with some of the other cues in the squares, playing the roles of student A and B alternately. Let the class work out the language they will need to respond to one another.

4 Doing the activity:
   ▶ Students fill out the chart with information about themselves.
   ▶ Students move around the classroom, talking to different classmates to get the information needed.
   ▶ Whenever they find someone who has something in common with them, they must write that person's name in the corresponding square. **Note:** One different name per square.
   ▶ The first person to fill all the squares with different names says *Bingo!*, and wins. Alternatively, stop the activity after a certain period of time and check who has filled the largest number of squares.

Variation

You may want to use this activity to review any material before a test or as you begin a new level. The questions need not be related to one specific topic or cover any specific grammar point.

Note on class size

If you are working with fewer than ten students in class, allow them to repeat the names in the squares two or three times. Alternatively, let them work in pairs and see which pair has the most things in common.

birthday (month)	colour of toothbrush 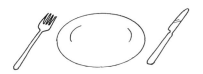	favourite food
You: _____	You: _____	You: _____
And: _____	And: _____	And: _____

age of parents (age of one of them)	place of residence (neighbourhood)	number of brothers and sisters
You: _____	You: _____	You: _____
And: _____	And: _____	And: _____

last name (number of letters)	come to class (means of transport) 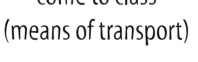	phone number (the last digit)
You: _____	You: _____	You: _____
And: _____	And: _____	And: _____

Find people who have things in common with you:
- write your own answers
- talk to your classmates

How much do you have in common with the other students?

10.2 What's my answer?

Language focus

Yes/no questions with present simple

Level

Beginner or elementary

Type

Betting game

Topic

Open

Interaction

Groups of two to six

Time

15–20 minutes

Material

Set of cards (one per group)

Vocabulary

Verb *be* and other vocabulary items generated by students.

Comments

This game is excellent for learners to understand and master yes/no questions with *be* and other verbs, plus short answers with auxiliaries, with particular attention on the *be* and *do* contrast. This means they may ask and answer yes/no questions in the present simple, present continuous and/or future with *going to*. It is also a lot of fun to play, because it involves betting and tests how well acquainted learners are with one another.

Language output

A: *Are you an English teacher?*
B: *No, I'm not.*
A: *Do you go to the movies every week?*
B: *Yes, I do.*

Procedures

1 Before class, cut out one set of cards for every group.

2 Recap yes/no questions by writing a few short answers with *be* and *do* on the board, and eliciting correct and appropriate questions for them.

3 Demonstrate the game by taking a card (e.g. *Yes, we do*) and asking the class a question that will yield the answer on your card (e.g. *Do we have class on (day of the week when you actually have class)?*). When they have given you the answer, show them the card and tell them you can discard it. Then, pick another card (e.g. *Yes, we are*) and ask the class a question that will **not** yield the desired answer (e.g. *Are you English teachers?*). As they answer *No, we aren't*, show them the card and tell them you cannot discard it.

4 Divide the class into groups and hand out the material.

5 Playing the game:

▶ Players shuffle and deal out the cards evenly, disregarding any cards left over.

▶ The first player picks one of his or her cards, and thinks of a question that will yield the answer on that card. He or she then tries to guess who in the group will give him or her the answer on the card, and directs the question to that person.

▶ If the respondent produces a short answer that equals the one on the card, the player may discard it; if not, he or she keeps the card.

▶ Players take turns proceeding in this way. The first player to get rid of all of his or her cards wins the game.

Variation

You may use this game to practise other contrasts, such as simple past v. present perfect simple. All you have to do is produce a new set of cards containing the appropriate short answers with *did, have* and *has*.

Note on class size

The ideal group size for playing this game is four. If your class is very small, you may have students play it in pairs, but it will not be as much fun. For a very large class, use groups of six and have them play it twice.

Yes, I am.	Yes, he is.	Yes, she is.
Yes, it is.	Yes, we are.	Yes, they are.
Yes, I do.	Yes, he does.	Yes, she does.
Yes, it does.	Yes, they do.	No, I'm not.
No, he isn't.	No, she isn't.	No, we aren't.
No, they aren't.	No, I don't.	No, he doesn't.
No, she doesn't.	No, it doesn't.	No, they don't.

10.3 All about us

Language focus

Wh- questions with mixed tenses

Level

Any

Type

Personal trivia

Topic

Open/personal

Interaction

Groups of three or four

Time

20–30 minutes

Material

Set of slips (one per group)

Vocabulary

Wh- words *what, what kind, what time, when, where, who, why, how, how long, how often, how many, how much*

Comments

This personalized trivia pursuit can be used at any level for intensive practice with wh- question formation, as the questions are totally generated by the students. The wh- words can be combined with any vocabulary and verb forms they have learned. It is therefore also excellent for reviewing purposes. Finally, it helps learners to become better acquainted with one another.

Language output

A: *What kind of movies does (name) like?*
B: *He/she likes westerns and thrillers.*
A: *How long has (name) been married?*
B: *He/she has been married for five years.*

Procedures

1 Before class, cut out one set of slips for every group.

2 Go over question formation and model the language several times with the whole class.

3 Playing the game:

▶ Each group writes questions about the members of one other group, plus the answers, in the appropriate spaces on the slips. Then, they fold the bottom of each slip so as to conceal the answers, and pass them around following the diagram below:

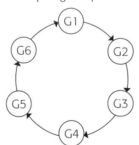

Preparing the questions

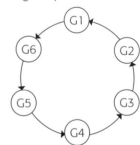

Passing the questions around

▶ Now players compete with one another within their groups. They take turns drawing a slip and reading the question on it. Whoever knows the answer puts their hand up and answers. The answer is checked against the one written at the bottom of the slip. If it is correct, the respondent gets the slip; if not, someone else may try. In case no one knows, the player who reads out the question discloses the answer and sets the slip aside.

▶ When all the questions have been asked, players count their slips. Whoever has the largest number of slips wins the game.

Variation

If your students are not very well acquainted with one another, set another context, e.g. famous people, world knowledge, etc.

What .... ?	Where .... ?
Answer: fold here	*Answer:* fold here

When .... ?	Who .... ?
Answer: fold here	*Answer:* fold here

Why .... ?	How long .... ?
Answer: fold here	*Answer:* fold here

How often .... ?	How much .... ?
Answer: fold here	*Answer:* fold here

How many .... ?	How .... ?
Answer: fold here	*Answer:* fold here

What kind .... ?	What time .... ?
Answer: fold here	*Answer:* fold here

10.4 Unique me

Language focus

Auxiliaries, *too, either, so, neither*

Level

Elementary to intermediate

Type

Sharing

Topic

Open/personal

Interaction

Groups of two to four

Time

10–15 minutes

Material

Set of cards (one per group)

Vocabulary

Auxiliaries: *be, do, can*

Comments

Expressing agreement and disagreement is an important function in communication, but by no means easy in English as it involves good control of a complex auxiliary system, plus contrasting elements such as *too, either, so, neither*. This student-centred activity has been designed to provide practice with these points while giving learners plenty of room to talk about themselves.

Language output

A: *I just love Michael Jackson.*
B: *I do too. / So do I. / Well, I don't.*
A: *I really can't sing at all.*
B: *I can't either. / Neither can I. / Well, I can.*

Procedures

1 Before class, cut out one set of cards for every group.

2 On the board, write down a few statements similar to those on the cards. Elicit possible endings from half of the class. From the other half, elicit agreement and disagreement, drawing their attention to the correct use of the target language.

3 Playing the game:
   ▶ Players shuffle the cards and deal them out evenly.
   ▶ Whoever gets the card *I just love* … begins the game by completing the sentence with some content about him or herself that he or she believes no one else will be able to echo with *too/so* or *either/neither*.
   ▶ All the other players then respond with agreement or disagreement. If no *too/so* or *either/ neither* responses are produced, then the first player 'wins' the card for his or her 'uniqueness', by laying it next to him or herself. Otherwise, the card goes to the centre of the table.
   ▶ Players take turns proceeding in this way. Note that the group may challenge anyone's statement if they think it is untrue. You will want this to happen as it generates conversation.
   ▶ The game ends when all the cards have been used. Whoever has the largest number of cards laid next to him or herself wins the game.

Note on language output

You may want to leave out inversion with *so/neither* when working with elementary learners.

Variation

For intermediate or more advanced groups, use ***Unique me II***. It has been designed to provide practice with a wider range of auxiliaries, inversion with *so/neither*, and possessives, e.g. *A: My mother is scared of snakes, B: So is mine*, as we have often observed learners struggling with this kind of construction.

I just love...

I don't...

I can... very well.

I really can't...

Tomorrow I am...

I am not a good...

Last night I...

Yesterday I didn't...

I often...

I'm not going...

I would like...

I was...

I have always...

I have never...

I'd rather...

I would never...

I used to... when...

I couldn't...

Next year I will...

I don't have to...

I hate it when...

I can't stand....

My favourite subject at school...

My mother...

11.1 Come one, come all

Language focus

a/an v. *some*

Level

Beginner or elementary

Type

Board game

Topic

Food

Interaction

Groups of two to six

Time

15–20 minutes

Material

Board and dice (one per group), worksheet and counters (one per student)

Vocabulary

Nouns: *pizza, bread, coffee/tea, cheese, sausage roll, grapes, ice-cream, apple, strawberries, lemonade, croissant, biscuits, cake, hot-dog, wine, hamburger, pie, beer, soup*

Partitives (optional): *a piece of, a slice of, a glass of, a cup of*

Comments

Your beginner or elementary students will certainly enjoy this contextualized board game where they will be able to practise the use of *a/an* v. *some* with countable and uncountable nouns. It is interactive throughout, and the luck factor will play down on competition, thus encouraging weaker learners to participate without fear.

Language output

A: *Would you like a hot-dog / some wine / some strawberries?*
B: *Yes, please. / No, thanks.*

Procedures

1 Before class: We have provided you with two identical copies of the same worksheet on a single page to save you photocopies. So, get only half as many photocopies of the page as you have students in the class, and cut the page in half as indicated.

2 In class, hand out one half of the worksheet to each student, and elicit the articles/partitives for the nouns given. Alternatively, pair off students, let them put in the articles/partitives, and check with the whole class.

3 On the board, write the skeleton for the dialogue in ***Language output*** above. Model the language a couple of times.

4 Set the context by telling your class: *You are going to an end-of-term party. Before going, decide what you want to have there. Tick the five items that you want.*

5 Have students individually select the five different things they would like to have at the party.

6 Playing the game:
  ▸ Players place their counters at START.
  ▸ The first player casts the dice and moves his or her counter accordingly. The person to his or her right then offers him or her the item in the square where the counter has landed. If the item is among those previously selected by the player, he or she accepts it and ticks it off his or her list. If not, he or she simply declines.
  ▸ Players take turns proceeding in this way until everyone has moved round the board once. Then, players count the items they have each ticked off their lists. The player who had the largest number of items he or she wanted wins the game.

Variation

Replace the pictures on the board with others depicting the most popular foods and beverages served at parties in your country.

Note on material

If students are playing in groups of two or three, give them coins instead of dice, and have them select eight items instead of five. By moving one square (heads) or two squares (tails) and working with a larger number of items, they will get more practice.

From *Games for Grammar Practice* © Cambridge University Press 2000 **PHOTOCOPIABLE**

Come one, come all

1 Before the party.
Are you hungry? thirsty? Circle the things you would like to have at the party.

_____ cheese	_____ hot-dogs
_____ sausage rolls	_____ wine
_____ grapes	_____ hamburgers
_____ ice-cream	_____ pie
_____ apples	_____ beer
_____ strawberries	_____ soup
_____ lemonade	_____ pizza
_____ croissants	_____ bread
_____ biscuits	_____ coffee
_____ cake	

2 At the party.
Tick the things from your list as you get them.

3 After the party.
How many things did you get? Are you still hungry or thirsty?

Come one, come all

1 Before the party.
Are you hungry? thirsty? Circle the things you would like to have at the party.

_____ cheese	_____ hot-dogs
_____ sausage rolls	_____ wine
_____ grapes	_____ hamburgers
_____ ice-cream	_____ pie
_____ apples	_____ beer
_____ strawberries	_____ soup
_____ lemonade	_____ pizza
_____ croissants	_____ bread
_____ biscuits	_____ coffee
_____ cake	

2 At the party.
Tick the things from your list as you get them.

3 After the party.
How many things did you get? Are you still hungry or thirsty?

12.1 Pack 'n' go

Language focus

***There be* in present simple**

Level

Elementary

Type

Information pool

Topic

Hotels

Interaction

Pairs

Time

10–15 minutes

Material

Worksheets A and B
(one per student)

Vocabulary

Places: *supermarket, souvenir shop, restaurant, hamburger bar, cinema, disco, theatre, public pool, tennis court, newsstand, art gallery, museum, bar, gift shop, clothes shop, public library, bank, bookshop, fitness centre, hairdresser's, convenience store, bus stop, taxi stand, underground station, laundrette, photo shop, amusement park, ice-cream shop, post office, cashpoint*

Comments

This game offers learners contextualized and intensive practice with yes/no questions and short answers involving the use of *there is/are*. What is so appealing about this activity is that it is the learners who decide what will go on the worksheet, what questions to ask, and when they have obtained enough information to accomplish their task.

Language output

A: *Is there a supermarket near the hotel?*
B: *Yes, there is./No, there isn't (but there is a very good convenience store just across from the hotel).*
A: *Are there any restaurants near the hotel?*
B: *Yes, there are./No, there aren't.*

Procedures

1   Before class, photocopy the worksheet and cut the copies in half as indicated.

2   Go over the use of *there is/are* by asking the class about places near your school. Model the language several times.

3   Hand out worksheet A to half of the class, and worksheet B to the other half. Pair off students A and B.

4   Set the situation by telling your class: *Students A, you are hotel owners in your town. Students B, you are travelling to A's town.*

5   Doing the activity:

▶   Individually, students A write their names on the hotel roof, and decide what kind of places there are around their hotel by selecting eight items from the list and plotting them on the map. Items may be repeated, e.g. two hotels, three restaurants, etc.

▶   Individually, students B decide why they are travelling and who with (clarify vocabulary for these two parts of the worksheet if necessary). Having such specific circumstances in mind, they decide what will be important for them to have near the hotel by checking eight of the items listed on their worksheet.

▶   Students work in pairs, asking for and giving information according to the decisions they made in the previous steps.

▶   If student B thinks student A's hotel is not suitable, he or she should talk to other hotel owners until an appropriate one is found.

B TRAVELLER

You are going to spend about two or three weeks in A's town. Consider the following aspects of your trip.

1 You're travelling:
- [ ] on business
- [ ] on holiday
- [ ] to do a course
- [ ] to attend a series of conferences
- [ ] to visit relatives
- [ ] to visit friends
- [ ] to do research for school/work

2 You're travelling:
- [ ] alone
- [ ] with colleagues
- [ ] with classmates
- [ ] with family
- [ ] with friends
- [ ] with husband/wife
- [ ] others _____

You would like the hotel to be near (tick eight items):
- [ ] supermarket
- [ ] souvenir shops
- [ ] restaurants
- [ ] hamburger bars
- [ ] cinemas
- [ ] discos
- [ ] theatres
- [ ] public pool
- [ ] tennis court
- [ ] newsstand
- [ ] art galleries
- [ ] museums
- [ ] bars
- [ ] gift shop
- [ ] clothes shops
- [ ] public library
- [ ] bank
- [ ] bookshops
- [ ] fitness centre
- [ ] hairdresser's
- [ ] convenience store
- [ ] bus stop
- [ ] taxi stand
- [ ] underground station
- [ ] laundrette
- [ ] photo shop
- [ ] amusement park
- [ ] ice-cream shop
- [ ] post office
- [ ] cashpoint

Talk to your partner and find out if there are the eight items you have selected near his/her hotel.

Is A's hotel right for you?

A HOTEL OWNER

_____'S HOTEL

What is there near your hotel? Select eight items and place them on your map.

1 supermarket
2 souvenir shops
3 restaurants
4 hamburger bars
5 cinemas
6 discos
7 theatres
8 public pool
9 tennis court
10 newsstand
11 art galleries
12 museums
13 bars
14 gift shop
15 clothes shops
16 public library
17 bank
18 bookshops
19 fitness centre
20 hairdresser's
21 convenience store
22 bus stop
23 taxi stand
24 underground station
25 laundrette
26 photo shop
27 amusement park
28 ice-cream shop
29 post office
30 cashpoint

From *Games for Grammar Practice* © Cambridge University Press 2001 **PHOTOCOPIABLE**

91

12.2 Rain or shine

Language focus

It as subject

Level

Intermediate

Type

Tic-tac-toe

Topic

Weather conditions

Interaction

Teams of two or three

Time

10–15 minutes

Material

Grid and set of cards (one for every two teams)

Vocabulary

Weather conditions: *cold, hot, windy, cloudy, foggy, raining, snowing, freezing, sunny*

Adjectives: *difficult, easy, hard, impossible, dangerous, safe, expensive, cheap, interesting, exciting, sensible, silly, important, nice, stupid, crazy*

Comments

This game provides practice with the dummy subject *it* for verbs and adjectives related to the weather, as well as adjectives that may take an infinitive clause as a complement. These structures often pose difficulties for learners whose native language allows for zero subjects. The game focuses on form and accuracy, but also requires creativity, strategy and cooperation within teams.

Language output

When it's foggy, it's dangerous to drive on the motorway.
It's silly to spend the day indoors when it is sunny outside.

Procedures

1 Before class, separate one grid (top half) for every two teams. Then, cut out the adjective cards (bottom half) and put them inside a bag or envelope, one set for every two teams.

2 In class, take one verb or adjective from the grid and one adjective from the cards. Write them on the board with an example of your own, as shown in **Language output**. Elicit a few more examples from the class, drawing their attention to the target structures.

3 Divide the class into teams, pair off teams, and hand out the material.

4 Playing the game:
  ▶ Objective of the game: to form a vertical, horizontal or diagonal row of correct answers on the grid (tic-tac-toe).
  ▶ Teams appoint one player to time the responses and keep the score.
  ▶ Team A picks a card from the bag or envelope, and chooses one slot in the grid. Before their time is up (let's say, one or two minutes), they must produce a sentence using the word in the slot and the adjective on the card, as shown in **Language output**.
  ▶ If their sentence is accepted by everyone in terms of meaning and form, they mark the chosen slot as their own.
  ▶ Teams take turns proceeding in this way until one of them does tic-tac-toe, in which case they score one point, or until all slots have been taken without either of them doing tic-tac-toe.
  ▶ Have them play the game several times. When you think they have had enough practice, have them add up their points. The team with the highest score wins the game.

Note on material

As students will be playing the game several times, they may either use different symbols to mark their slots in each round, or copy the grid, which is easy and quick to do.

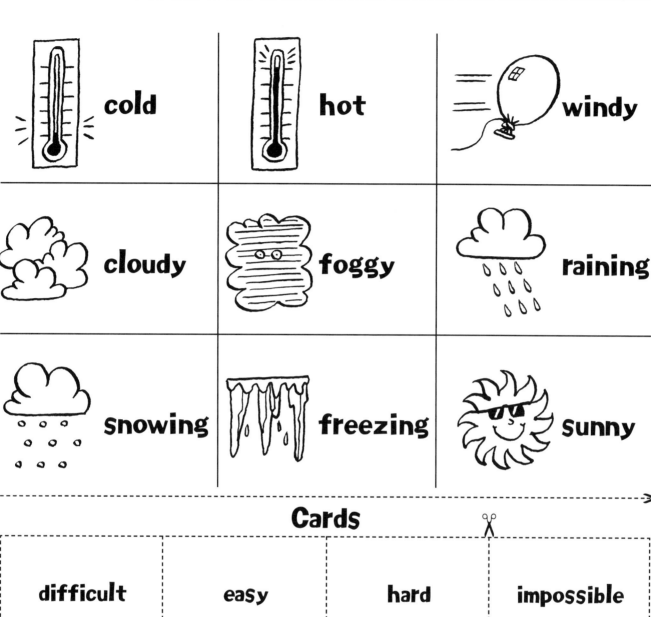

cold

hot

windy

cloudy

foggy

raining

snowing

freezing

sunny

Cards

difficult	easy	hard	impossible
dangerous	safe	expensive	cheap
interesting	exciting	sensible	silly
important	nice	stupid	crazy

13.1 Verb trap

Language focus

To v. -ing

Level

Intermediate

Type

Grid game

Topic

Open

Interaction

Groups of three or four

Time

15–20 minutes

Material

Grid (one per group), coloured pencils (one per student)

Vocabulary

Verb + gerund: *enjoy, practise, miss, start, love, can't stand, remember, regret, can't help, admit (to), postpone, try, avoid, stop, keep, imagine, mind, consider, hate*

Verb + infinitive: *decide, manage, start, promise, threaten, love, attempt, remember, try, tend, seem, stop, learn, forget, refuse, hate*

Comments

This fun and challenging game focuses on the accurate use of verb + gerund or infinitive, important patterns that learners must attend to. However, winning the game is also a result of strategy and cunning. In addition, learners take full responsibility for peer correction.

Language output

Please stop making all that noise.
I stopped to have a snack on my way to class.

Procedures

1 Take some of the verbs followed by the gerund and others by the infinitive from the grid. Ask your class to make sentences with them, requiring that they be followed by another verb. Draw their attention to the use of gerunds and infinitives. Don't forget to go over those verbs that may take either a gerund or an infinitive as a complement, but with a difference in meaning.

2 Divide the class into groups and hand out the material. Players in each group should use different coloured pencils.

3 Playing the game:

   ◗ Objective of the game: to occupy as many hexagons as possible while, at the same time, trying to prevent the advance of opponents.

   ◗ To start the game, each player chooses one hexagon and makes a sentence with the verb in it. If the sentence is judged correct by the rest of the group, the player may claim the hexagon as his or her own by marking it with the coloured pencil. **Note:** To maintain a reasonable pace, set a time limit for the players to come up with their sentences.

   ◗ From then on, a player's target hexagon must be contiguous with any hexagon already occupied by him or her. **Note:** Because of this rule, players may use the following strategy: they may move into the hexagons that are contiguous with their opponents', thus isolating them and preventing them from occupying new hexagons.

   ◗ The game proceeds until all the hexagons have been taken. Each player counts the hexagons he or she occupies. Whoever has the largest number wins the game.

Note on class size

Even if your class is small, do not let students play in pairs. This will cancel out the strategic factor, resulting in a very dull game!

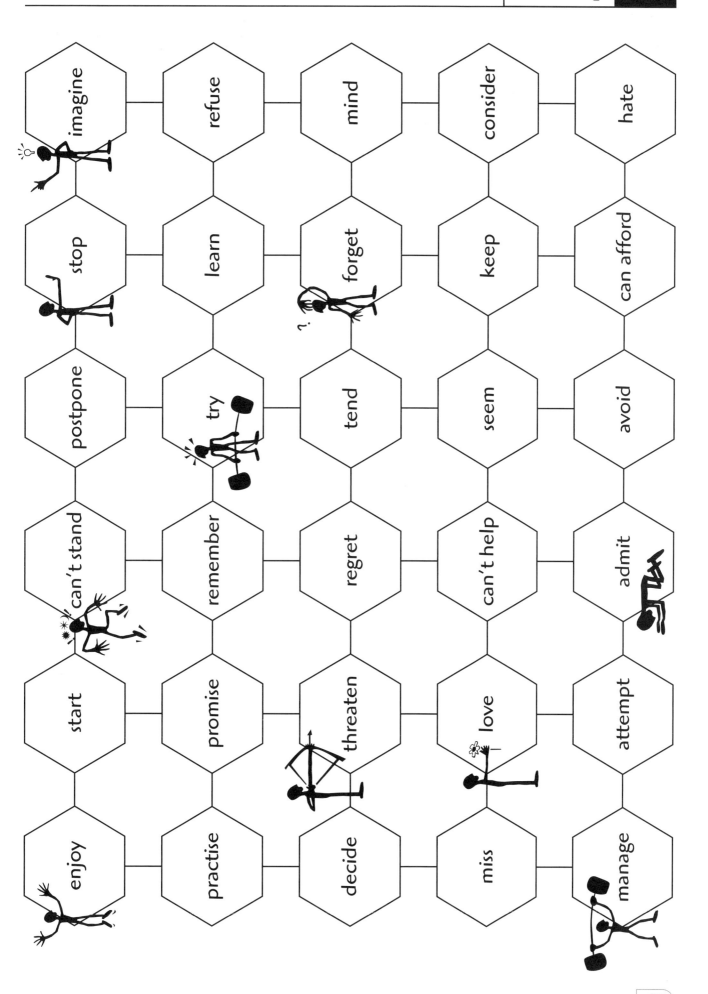

14.1

The preposition contest

Language focus

Prepositions of place and time

Level

Beginner

Type

Tic-tac-toe

Topic

Open

Interaction

Teams of two to four

Time

15 minutes

Material

Grid and set of cards (one per group)

Vocabulary

Adverbials of place and time: *at work, home, midday, 8 o'clock, school, night, the City Bank, Harrods, the beach; on December 25th, Sunday, holiday, the wall, my birthday, 5th Avenue, the beach, the second floor, the radio; in my apartment, class, Book 1, New York, July, the morning, the summer, this neighbourhood*

Comments

This game gives beginners an opportunity to practise or review prepositions of place and time. Here, luck plays down the knowledge factor, which motivates weaker learners to participate without fear. The game also encourages cooperation within teams and peer correction across teams.

Language output

My parents are at home now.
My birthday is on May 5th.

Procedures

1 Before class, separate one grid (top half) for every two teams. Then, cut out the cards (bottom half) and put them into bags or envelopes, again one set for every two teams.

2 In class, review the use of prepositions to form adverbials of time and place, as well as some fixed expressions.

3 Divide the class into teams, pair off teams, and hand out the material.

4 Playing the game:

▶ Objective of the game: to make grammatically correct sentences in order to form a vertical, horizontal or diagonal row of X's or O's (tic-tac-toe).

▶ Team A (X) picks a card from the bag or envelope, on which they will find a phrase. Next, they choose a slot in the grid containing the preposition that they think will form a correct adverbial with the phrase on the card. They then make a sentence with the adverbial.

▶ If the sentence is judged correct by everyone, team A marks the slot with an X; otherwise, they do not score.

▶ Team B (O) proceeds in the same way.

▶ The two teams take turns drawing the cards and making sentences. The game will end either when one of the teams does tic-tac-toe, or when all the slots have been taken but neither team has done tic-tac-toe, in which case it is a draw. **Note:** In case a team picks a card for which all the correct prepositions (slots) have been taken, they put it back inside the bag or envelope and draw another one.

▶ They may play this game several times. In that case, each team scores one point every time they do tic-tac-toe. When the activity is over, they count their points, and the team with the highest score wins.

Variation

When making your own version, you may want to leave one slot blank for words like *last, next, downtown, here, there,* etc., which take no preposition.

Note on material

As students will probably be playing several times, either have them mark their slots with different symbols every time they play, or have them copy the grid.

GRID

ON	IN	ON
IN	AT	AT
AT	ON	IN

CARDS

work	home	midday	8 o'clock	school
December 25th	Sunday	holiday	the wall	my birthday
my apartment	class	Book 1	New York	July
the morning	the summer	this neighbourhood	night	the City Bank
Harrods	5th Avenue	the beach	the second floor	the radio

14.2 You and I

Language focus

Adjective + preposition

Level

Intermediate

Type

Sharing

Topic

Personality and feelings

Interaction

Pairs

Time

15–30 minutes

Material

Worksheet (one per student)

Vocabulary

Adjectives + prepositions: *scared of, good at, proud of, interested in, fed up with, annoyed about, jealous of, responsible for, different from, hopeless at, used to, tired of*

Comments

This game makes learners attend to and practise adjective + preposition combinations, as well as the position of prepositions in questions and relative clauses, a point that most learners find it difficult to grasp. Because it invites participants to find out more about their classmates and talk about themselves, it is also excellent for class bonding.

Language output

A: *What is something you are really scared of?*
B: *I'm really scared of spiders. What about you?*
A: *I'm scared of snakes.*
B: *Why? Have you ever been bitten by a snake? / How do you react when you see one?*

Procedures

1 Write the adjectives from the worksheet on the board and elicit the prepositions they go with and the kinds of complements the prepositions may take, i.e. nouns and gerunds. After that, model the language in **Language output** by formulating some questions, eliciting responses and engaging in conversation. Draw students' attention to the position of the prepositions.

2 Hand out the worksheets.

3 Doing the activity:

▶ Have students fill out the worksheets individually with information about themselves.

▶ Either pair off students, especially the ones you think are not yet very well acquainted with one another, or let them choose their partners.

▶ Participants choose six to eight of the questions on the worksheet to ask their partners and develop a conversation.

Variation

▶ If you want to turn this activity into a game, have students ask and answer all of the 12 questions and check the balloons where they have something in common with their partners. Then, with the whole class, find out which pair has the largest number of things in common. **Note:** This variation will, however, turn a fluency building activity into a race, as students will be focusing on finding out what they have in common with their partners rather than becoming better acquainted with one another.

▶ To challenge students a bit further, leave out the prepositions in the balloons and have students supply them in the preparation phase. This has the added plus of focusing on the position of prepositions.

▶ You may also have them report their findings with *Both … and I … / Neither I nor … / Both of us … / Neither of us …* etc.

Note on time

This activity may take anything from 15 to 30 minutes, depending on your students' level of interest and how much they engage in conversation to know one another better.

What's something you are really scared of?

What's something you are good at?

Who's someone you are very proud of?

What's something you are deeply interested in?

What's something you can easily get annoyed about?

What's something you are now fed up with?

Who's someone you are particularly jealous of?

What are you responsible for at home?

Who in your family are you very different from?

What are you hopeless at?

What can't you get used to?

What are you absolutely tired of?

14.3 Preposition checkers

Vocabulary

Verbs and prepositions: *shout, stare, smile, aim, throw AT; break, crash, drive, bump, turn INTO; discuss, enter, like, match, dare (ø = NO PREPOSITION); believe, specialize, succeed, trust, interfere IN; collide, cope, provide, supply, disagree WITH; dream, die, approve, accuse, remind OF; complain, explain, describe, apologize, give, object, submit, reply, respond, contribute TO; hear, suffer, borrow, protect, prevent, recover, retire, release, rescue, resign FROM; insist, count, depend, bet, spend, congratulate, comment, concentrate, rely, lean ON; criticize, blame, vote, ask, apply, prepare, charge, hope, beg, search FOR*

Note: Some of the verbs above may take other prepositions.

Comments

This game urges learners to attend to and practise verb + preposition combinations. It focuses on form, with learners in charge of peer correction. Strategy and luck are the two other elements that come into play in determining the winner.

Language output

I don't like it when someone shouts at me.
My uncle crashed into the front gate because he is a very bad driver.
My brother is applying for several jobs at the same time.

Procedures

1 Before class, cut out the cards and put them into bags or envelopes, one set for each group.

2 Take some of the verbs from the cards and write them on the board. Elicit the prepositions they go with and some meaningful sentences containing the verb+preposition combinations.

3 Divide the class into groups and hand out the material.

4 Playing the game:
  ▶ Players place their counters at 1, 2 or 3 on the board.
  ▶ Objective of the game: To move the counters across the board into the square with the corresponding number. Moves can be made into triangles sharing a side or vertex with the triangle where one's counter is or by jumping over an opponent's counter.
  ▶ Players take turns picking a card from the bag or envelope. If the verb on it goes with the preposition in any one of the possible target triangles (see above), the player makes a sentence with the verb+preposition combination. If the sentence is accepted as correct by the group, the player advances the counter into the target triangle. If, on the other hand, the sentence is judged incorrect by the group, the player remains in place. In neither case will the card go back into the bag or envelope.
  ▶ In case there is no match, the player may put the card back into the bag or envelope and pick one more. If there is again no match or the player produces an incorrect answer, he or she will put the card back and remain in place.
  ▶ The first player to bring his or her counter into the home position across the board wins the game.

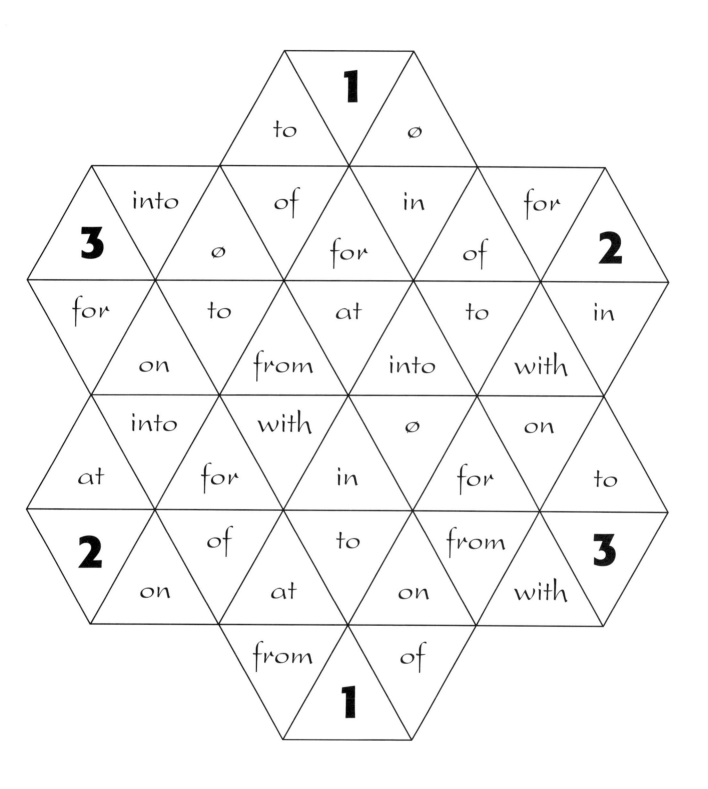

CARDS

shout	stare	smile	aim	throw
break	crash	drive	bump	turn
discuss	enter	like	match	dare
believe	specialize	succeed	trust	interfere
collide	cope	provide	supply	disagree
insist	count	depend	bet	spend
complain	explain	describe	apologize	give

CARDS

object	submit	reply	respond	contribute
hear	suffer	borrow	protect	prevent
recover	retire	release	rescue	resign
dream	die	approve	accuse	remind
congratulate	comment	concentrate	rely	lean
criticize	blame	vote	ask	apply
prepare	charge	hope	beg	search

15.1 How do they compare?

Language focus

Comparative forms
of adjectives

Level

Intermediate

Type

Dominoes

Topic

Open

Interaction

Groups of three to five

Time

20 minutes

Material

Set of dominoes
(one per group)

Vocabulary

Adjectives: prompted by dominoes.

Nouns: *(watching) TV, tortoise, rabbit, (going to the) theatre, (going to the) cinema, hourglass, alarm clock, cat, lion, (short/tall) woman, candle, light bulb, (glass of) wine, (mug of) beer, shopping bag/going shopping, suitcase/travelling, credit cards, cheque, (thin) woman, (fat) man, fishing, gardening, elephant, mouse, computer, calculator, hamburger, apple, (playing) cards, (playing) chess, E.T., Titanic, sun/sunny day, snowman/snow/winter, aeroplane, balloon, drum, violin, feather, anchor, man, woman, rugby, football, block of flats, house, bowling, tennis, (reading a) book*

Comments

In this game, learners are given an opportunity to practise the comparative forms of adjectives and to review or expand vocabulary as well. The game taps into their creativity as it requires them to find original comparisons to win the game. Peer correction and group discussion are also encouraged here.

Language output

A tortoise is slower than a rabbit.
Gardening is more tiring than fishing.
Cheques are not as convenient as credit cards.

Procedures

1 Before class, cut out the dominoes along the dotted lines as indicated, one set for each group.

2 Review the comparative forms of adjectives by writing the names of several items on the board and eliciting comparisons from your class. Include some examples with gerunds as subjects, e.g. *Watching TV is more relaxing than reading a book*, as students may want to use this kind of construction during the game.

3 Divide the class into groups and hand out the material.

4 Playing the game:
 ▶ Players shuffle the dominoes and deal them out as follows:
   5 players, 3 dominoes each   4 players, 4 dominoes each
   3 players, 5 dominoes each   2 players, 7 dominoes each
   The remaining dominoes are piled face down in the centre, except one, which is turned face up to begin the game with.
 ▶ In turns, players may discard their dominoes by placing them next to one of the two ends of the domino on the table, provided that they can either find a plausible comparison for the adjacent items depicted on the domino and express the comparison in a correct sentence. It is the group who decides whether a given sentence is acceptable or not.
 ▶ The game proceeds as in ordinary dominoes. The first player to discard all of his or her dominoes wins the game.

Variations

 ▶ Change the pictures on the dominoes to suit your learners' proficiency level.
 ▶ With more advanced learners, you may wish to encourage the use of intensifiers, e.g. *A tortoise is a lot slower than a rabbit, Gardening is far more tiring than fishing.*

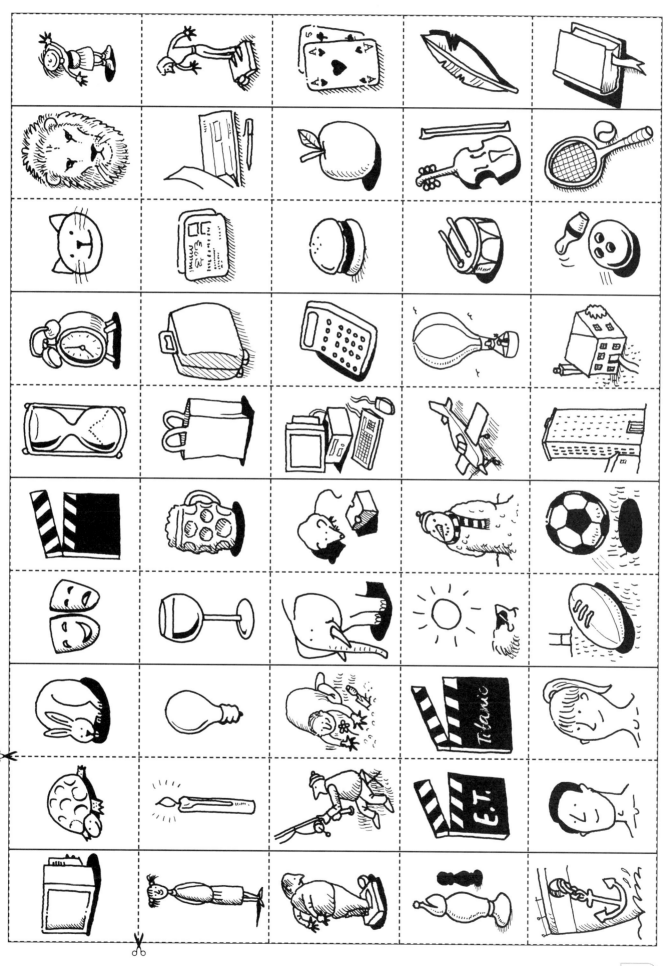

15.2 Three of a kind

Language focus

Comparative forms
of quantifiers

Level

Pre-intermediate

Type

Rummy

Topic

Common nouns

Interaction

Groups of three to six

Time

10–15 minutes

Material

Set of cards
(one per group)

Vocabulary

Countable nouns: *people, tools, women, scissors, glasses, mice*

Uncountable nouns: *pie, money, furniture, luggage, mail, water*

Comments

This game is an adaptation of Rummy designed to provide practice with the comparative forms of quantifiers: *more, less, fewer, as much as* and *as many as*. The pictures on the cards cover countable and uncountable nouns so as to help learners decide which quantifier forms to use.

Language output

There is more / less / as much furniture in this picture than/as in that one.

There are more / fewer / as many people in this picture than/as in that one.

Procedures

1 Before class, cut out the cards, one set for each group.

2 Using visual aids, elicit comparisons such as those shown in *Language output*, and model the language several times, making sure your learners understand how the countable/uncountable features of nouns determine the choice of quantifier form.

3 Divide the class into groups and hand out the material.

4 Playing the game:

  ❱ Players shuffle the cards and deal them out as follows: for three to four players, four cards each; and for five to six players, three cards each. The remaining cards are placed face down in the centre of the table.

  ❱ The first player picks a card from the table and tries to form sets of two or three of a kind. He or she then lays them on the table and makes one or more sentences comparing the items on them in terms of quantity, depending on how many cards he or she wishes to lay down.

  ❱ The next player picks a card from the pile. He or she may form new sets or complete whatever sets have already been laid on the table by other players, provided he or she produces sentences comparing the items on them. **Note:** If two cards depicting different quantities are laid down first, the player adding the third card to complete the set may either compare it unequally with one of the cards, or equally with the other.

  ❱ The first player to get rid of all of his or her cards wins the game.

Note on game rules

You will note that there is no rule preventing players from discarding cards when they produce incorrect sentences. You may either remind your students to do peer correction or make such a rule as a condition for discarding cards and, therefore, winning the game.

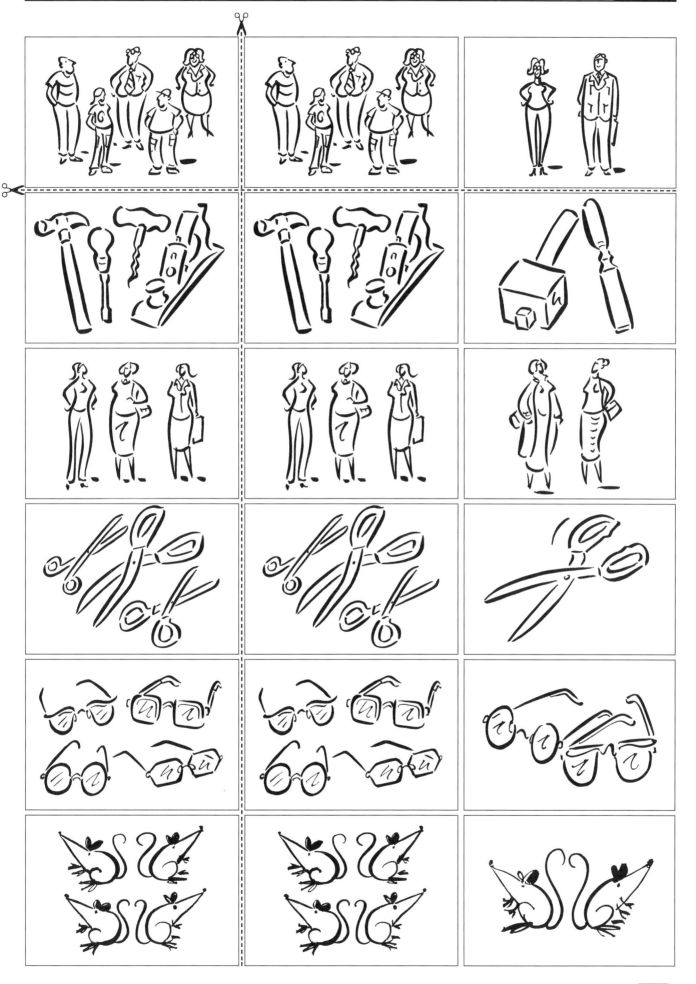

From *Games for Grammar Practice* © Cambridge University Press 2001 **PHOTOCOPIABLE**

16.1 Family album

Language focus

Subject pronouns and possessive adjectives

Level

Beginner

Type

Maze

Topic

Family

Interaction

Groups of three or four

Time

15 minutes

Material

Board and set of cards (one per group), counters (one per student)

Vocabulary

Subject pronouns: *I, you, he, she, it, we, they*

Possessive adjectives: *my, your, his, her, our, their*

Nouns related to: *family, school subjects, sports, entertainment*

Adjectives: *big, famous, busy, small, nice, comfortable, fantastic, favourite, pretty, intelligent, good, special*

Verbs: *be, have, work, do, play, live, come, visit, love, go, like, go out*

Adverbials: *very hard, on the phone, always, once a month, just across the street, together, every Saturday, usually*

Comments

This contextualized maze provides learners with an interesting and fun way to contrast and practise subject pronouns and possessive adjectives. In addition, it is rich in input in the form of statements, questions and vocabulary. Luck and strategy combine with language accuracy to determine the winner.

Language output

My parents are very busy people. They work very hard.
My brothers are my best friends. Their names are Carl and Cliff.

Procedures

1 Before class, cut out the cards and place them inside a bag or envelope, one set per group.

2 Divide the class into groups and hand out the material.

3 Model the language and demonstrate the basic principle of the game by drawing a card from one of the bags or envelopes, and asking the class where it could go. Repeat this a couple of times to make sure they can use the language correctly and have understood the principle of the game.

4 Playing the game:

  ◗ Objective of the game: to be the first to move from the top of the maze to the bottom.
  ◗ The first player draws a card. One of the following situations will then occur:
    a the player fills one of the slots in the four top squares correctly with the item on the card, in which case he or she may enter the maze by moving a counter into the target square;
    b the player knows that the item on the card does not fit into any of the top slots, in which case he or she may put it back into the bag or envelope and give it just one more try;
    c the player attempts to fill one of the slots, but produces a wrong sentence, in which case he or she puts the card back and remains in place.
  ◗ Players take turns proceeding in this way. After they have entered the maze, they may only move into those squares that are connected by a passageway to the square where their counter stands, and providing that the target square is not occupied by anyone else.
  ◗ The first player to come out of the maze wins the game.

Variation

You may follow the same procedures to practise other contrasts such as possessive adjectives and possessive pronouns, or any other grammar points. All you need is a new set of sentences and cards.

_____ name is Chuck. I am a student at Orange High.

Are _____ a student too?

_____ have a big family, two brothers and one sister, a dog and my cat Bernard.

This is my father. _____ is a police officer.

My parents are very busy people. _____ work very hard.

Does your mother work hard? What does _____ do?

My brothers are my best friends. _____ names are Carl and Cliff.

My brother Cliff plays in the school football team. _____ is the goalkeeper.

Do you have a brother? What's _____ name?

This is my sister. _____ name is Janet.

My sister is always on the phone with _____ boyfriend.

We live in Orange Garden. _____ is a small town but very nice.

_____ house is very nice and comfortable. We have a garden with beautiful flowers.

Do you and _____ family live in a house or an apartment?

My grandparents don't live in Orange Garden, but _____ come to visit once a month.

My grandmother is a fantastic cook. _____ chocolate cake is famous.

My family and I love the sea. _____ often go to the beach.

School is OK. _____ favourite subject is Maths. And I like Biology too.

This one is my English teacher. _____ name is David Palmer.

I have a girlfriend, Alice. _____ is very intelligent and pretty too.

These are David and Tim, my neighbours. _____ live just across the street.

David and I play tennis together at the club. _____ is a very good player.

My friends and I go out every Saturday. _____ usually go to parties or to a disco.

Today is a special day for me. _____ is my birthday.

MY	YOU	I	HE
THEY	SHE	THEIR	HE
HIS	HER	HER	IT
OUR	YOUR	THEY	HER
WE	MY	HIS	HER
THEY	HE	WE	IT

16.2 What a mess!

Vocabulary

Nouns: *(baseball) ball, crayons, train, backpack, sweater, skates, sunglasses, aeroplane, gloves, car*

Comments

This contextualized and task-oriented information gap activity is meant for practising -'s as an adjective and pronoun, plus questions with *whose*. The worksheet comes with illustrations so that learners may point at the objects while formulating questions about who they belong to. This, we have found, helps learners to focus on the meaning of their questions.

Language output

A: *Whose backpack is this?*
B: *That's Alice's (backpack).*
A: *And which group is Alice in?*
B: *She's in Linda's (group).*

Procedures

1 Before class, cut the worksheets in half as indicated. Reserve the top half (worksheet A) for half of the class, and the bottom half (worksheet B) for the other half of the class.

2 Using the worksheets, elicit and model the language in **Language output**. As you go along, build the skeleton on the board, because the target questions may still be difficult for elementary learners to handle all by themselves. Make sure they can understand and use the -'s both as an adjective and as a pronoun.

3 Pair off students with worksheets A and B.

4 Set the context and task by telling your class: *You are teaching assistants in a children's school. Check who the objects belong to and which group each child is in. Put the objects into the right boxes by writing the children's names below the boxes.*

5 Doing the activity:

▶ Students ask and answer the questions in **Language output** to pool the information they need to accomplish their task. As they obtain the information needed, they write down the children's names next to the objects they own and below the appropriate boxes.

▶ Together, students compare their decisions, that is, where they wrote the children's names.

A

Student	Group
Ben	Meggie
Eugene	Olivia
Greg	Olivia
Ivana	Meg
Kevin	Nancy

- ✂

B

Student	Group
Alice	Linda
Cindy	Nancy
Frank	Meg
Hector	Linda
Jane	Linda

  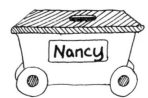 

Answers

Possible answers: page 59

	people		birds		sing.
	a kangaroo		a flea		jump.
	a monkey		a squirrel		climb trees.
	a penguin		a duck		swim.
Both	a cat	and	an owl	can	see in the dark.
	a child		a parrot		speak / imitate voices.
	an aeroplane		Superman		fly.
	a gun		a knife		kill.
	a turtle		a tree		live very long.
	a Porsche		a cheetah		run/go very fast.

Possible answers: page 70

Forks and coins		made of metal.
Tennis and squash		played with a racket.
Coffee and cotton		grown in tropical regions.
Polar bears and penguins		found in the Poles.
Shoes and socks		worn on our feet.
Presents and greeting cards	are	given at Christmas.
A bottle opener and a corkscrew		used to open bottles.
Paints and brushes		used for painting.
Glass and cement		made from sand.
A shower cap and a credit card		made of plastic.
Newspapers and magazines		found/bought/sold at the newsstand.
Stamps and airletters		found/bought/sold at the post office.